"Funny, poignant, and heartwarming, WriterMom Tales is a delight to read. Cornelia's stories are a beautiful reminder for moms like me to slow down in the busyness of life and be more intentional about taking time to enjoy my kids."
– **Melanie Dobson**, former corporate publicity manager for Focus on the Family, and author of *Love Finds You in Homestead, Iowa* and *The Silent Order.*

"Spiritual common sense for parenting, written with style and humor." – **Mike Thaler,** Zondervan author of *The Preacher Creature Strikes on Sunday* and creator of *The Black Lagoon* children's book series.

"As a real life mother of five, Cornelia has mastered the fine art of taking you into the complex world of motherhood and brilliant storytelling. Her stories are inspiring, thought provoking, and just plain fun to read. Cornelia takes you on the journey where love and hope is found in that special place called family." – **LouAnn Edwards**, mother of six, talk show host, award-winning humor writer, and author of *Don't Make me Laugh, can't you see I'm in the middle of a crisis?*

"In an age when society seems confused about what a real mom looks like, Cornelia is re-calibrating us to authentic Motherhood. Not only does she write with wit, grace and humor, she is communicating some of the most profound principles and practices of what it means to be a Mom. There is something that resonates with our soul and conscience: this is true, authentic and foundational to our families."
– **Dale Ebel**, founding pastor, Rolling Hills Community Church and founder, Dale Ebel Ministries.

"Cornelia is not only an extraordinarily dedicated mom and writer who brings an equal mix of bliss and ambition to the home front, she is an extraordinarily generous spirit. Writing about parenthood in a way that both informs and inspires, she changes lives through her written words and example."
– **Midge Pierce**, Media consultant and mom

WriterMom Tales

WriterMom Tales

Corralling the Commotion while Savoring the
Chaos, Spilled Cheerios, and Prayers
of Real-Life Motherhood

Dec. 2010

Bea and Family ~ Celebrating the gift of motherhood, family, friendship and life, given by the Creator!

Cornelia Becker Seigneur

I'll always treasure your friendship —
Cornelia

WriterMom Tales

www.corneliaseigneur.com

Cover and interior design by:
Dennis Marcellino and
Cornelia Becker Seigneur

Published by Creekside Publishing

Library of Congress Cataloging-in-Publication Data

Seigneur, Cornelia Becker.
  WriterMom tales : corralling the commotion while savoring the chaos, spilled Cheerios, and prayers of real-life motherhood / Cornelia Becker Seigneur.
    p. cm.
  ISBN 978-0-945272-49-6 (pbk. : alk. paper)
  1. Motherhood--Religious aspects--Christianity. 2. Parenting--Religious aspects--Christianity. 3. Families--Religious aspects--Christianity. 4. Parenting--United States--Anecdotes. 5. Motherhood--United States--Anecdotes. 6. Seigneur, Cornelia Becker--Anecdotes. 7. Mothers--United States--Anecdotes. I. Title. II. Title: Writer mom tales.
  BV4529.18.S45 2010
  248.8'431--dc22

                              2010031854

*This book is dedicated to God, and
to my five beautiful children,
Rachel Marianna, Ryan Christopher,
Wesley David, Mickael Josef,
and Augustin Heinz Martin,
so you'll always know how I feel about you
and about being your mom. And about life.*

*This book is also for other moms
who are trying to live out
the adventure and gift of motherhood
as designed by the Creator.*

CONTENTS

Acknowledgements

I am grateful to The Oregonian for publishing my Real-Life Mom column in the Southwest Weekly from 2005 to 2008, and to my editor Amy Wang, for believing in the idea. And, I offer thanks to The West Linn Tidings, where my On the Home Front/WriterMom column was published from 1999-2005. I am humbled by then-Tidings Publisher, the late Bob Bigelow, who, after reading my column, "Cherishing the Treasures Along the Road of Life," insisted I be paid for my mom columns. Many of the essays and columns in this collection first appeared in one form or another in one of these two newspapers from 1999-2008. And, I'll always be grateful to my first editor at The Oregonian's South Weekly, Pat Mullarkey, who first helped me realize my dream to write for the paper in 1996.

Thanks to Dawn Stanton, Sam Greengard, Jennifer Priest Mitchell, Kathy Conrad, Jeanie Higinbotham, and

Marupong Chuladul for being another set of eyes on parts of this project and general writing support. I value my West Linn writers group and my Rolling Hills writers' connection for their camaraderie.

And, I am so appreciative of Dennis Marcellino for his incredible patience while offering his professional assistance in book cover and interior design help, as well as publishing connections.

I am grateful for my parents Margit and Helmut Becker, and my in-laws Nancy and David Seigneur for their encouragement of my writing; and I thank my sister Sieglinde and brother Martin for allowing me to share stories. I am honored by so many people who have acknowledged me as a writer. I think of Judi Hickman, Faith Carter, Bea Hansen, Kelly Taylor, Kristi Easterlin, Dale Ebel, Liz Wainwright, Bev Hislop and my family and other friends who have said words of encouragement about my writing. And, my readers over the years have offered feedback, which I truly value.

Ultimately, I am eternally grateful to God and to His Son Jesus Christ, who gave us the gift of life and creativity.

Finally, I am humbled by my family's support of my writing. I thank my husband Chris for his ongoing understanding of my literary pursuits. And, I am especially blessed with the gift of my five sweet children, Rachel, Ryan, Wesley, Mickael Josef and Augustin, who are the reason I am a WriterMom.

"I am a collector of words. I love the way words and phrases and sentences and statements and paragraphs swirl together to make literary art."

– Cornelia Becker Seigneur

"Live the questions." – **Rainer Maria Rilke**

"I considered my ways, and turned my feet to your testimonies." – **Psalm 119: 59**

"I went to the woods because I wished to live deliberately, to front only the essential facts of life, and see if I could not learn what it had to teach, and not, when I came to die, discover that I had not lived." – **Henry David Thoreau**

"I had always felt life first as a story—and if there is a story there is a story teller."– **G.K. Chesterton**

"Hope is the thing with feathers
That perches in the soul
And sings the tune without the words
And never stops at all." – **Emily Dickinson**

"There is no greatness where there is no simplicity, goodness and truth." – **Leo Tolstoy**

"I am a little pencil in the hand of a writing God who is sending a love letter to the world." – **Mother Teresa**

Introduction

As a real mom of five children, far away from Hollywood, I find it hard to relate to the parenting messages of highly publicized movie star moms. They have nannies, housekeepers, and professional chefs at their beck and call. And, the Desperate Housewives on television scheme against their friends' husbands and children, while eyeing the neighbor's plumber. And, we've all tired of parenting publications where expert psychologists offer easy solutions to keeping children squabble-free, and kitschy mom books tell us how to be happy.

While Hollywood life may prove entertaining, the inescapable reality for most moms is a far cry from the bright lights of Los Angeles. And I've found that moms these days want more depth to parenting issues than the so-called experts' recycled 5-step plans to perfect families. Let's face it -- motherhood is hard, and moms need to know it is okay to admit that they crave quiet now and then. You love your kids but parenting can be difficult.

That's where *WriterMom Tales* comes in to offer a fresh take on being a mom. Reading this book is like talking to a trusted friend, who overlooks spilled Cheerios and invites you in for coffee and shared stories, somehow seeing the beauty in the chaos. What I've discovered is we learn best through story: networking with mom friends, talking with seasoned parents and grandparents, and gleaning life lessons from everyday life. And lots of praying and Scripture.

While reading *WriterMom Tales*, which is packed with a variety of real life experiences -- such as boys turning pieces of a wooden Nativity set into action figures at Christmas; chasing twin toddlers at the video store while trying to remain calm; the whirlwind that ensues when the UPS man arrives as kids step off the school bus; climbing with kids on trees fallen over creeks during hikes; muddling through the family dinner hour; handing over the car keys to a teenager for the first time; and speeding too often until we meet an elderly gentleman whose daily waving at cars reminds us of a slower era -- moms will recognize their own personal stories.

This book offers an honest look at the lessons of parenting—from late night homework sessions with kids when you'd sometimes rather be reading your own book, to the un-vacuumed carpet that becomes painfully visible when a friend stops by. *WriterMom Tales* provides the perspective of a real life mom in the real world, far away from a Hollywood script. The mom next door like you, the one who does her own dishes, washes her own laundry, prepares meals from scratch (okay, at times it's a jar of Ragu on angel hair), carts kids around, works two jobs, tries to teach kids lessons, reads to her children, takes her kids to church, and prays with her children before tucking them in, and drops into bed at night exhausted, with a book opened to the same page from the night before.

WriterMom Tales extracts the delightful ways children teach us life lessons, and presents a vulnerable voice of the sometimes uncertainty, worry, and guilt that can accompany motherhood. While *WriterMom Tales* saddles the tornado on the home front, it ultimately glimpses the beauty and reminds moms of the extraordinarily significant role God has designed for them in the lives of their children.

The individual essays found in *WriterMom Tales* are perfect for busy moms to savor one at a time, between children's naps, carpools, and taking kids to the dentist. The stories offer insight, faith, hope, humor, and prayers for the sometimes frustrating, but always beautiful adventure called motherhood.

GATHERING WORDS

"Fill your paper with the breathings of your heart."
— William Wordsworth

Fusing Literary Art and Motherhood

As I write this essay for my Real-Life Mom column for The Oregonian newspaper, my 4-year-old son, Augustin, sits on my shoulders with his legs wrapped around my neck and his arms around my head, swaying back and forth.

I have been home all day with my sweet, brown-eyed preschooler, who is sick today, but by the show of energy he is displaying, I believe his words, "I am better now, Mommy."

Today was originally supposed to be a full writing day for me. After preschool at Gladstone First Baptist Church, his Grandma Nancy was scheduled to pick him up so I could work.

With my family column to pen this week and a feature story due next week, along with a lineup of other ongoing projects, I needed the uninterrupted interval. Plus, I have to make dinner, attend my daughter's track meet later, prepare for the church Youth Group Bible study I lead tonight, and get ready for a Thursday home school writing class I teach at church.

But then being a WriterMom throws a curveball. After returning from my 5:30 a.m. power walk this morning with my friend Shelley, I find Augustin throwing up in the bathroom, then deal with other signs of the stomach flu, and my visions of a quiet day writing alone vanish.

"I guess I cannot go to preschool today, Mommy," Augustin announces. After canceling grandma and getting our four other children off to school, I settle in for a different kind of work: cleaning up vomit, washing blankets drenched in vomit, and helping my child dash to the bathroom on time to avoid mopping up a mess; all the while catching moments to write here and there, as is often the case for me.

The fine art of juggling motherhood with wearing other hats calls for creative measures.

People often ask me when I find time to write and I say, "Early mornings; between naps, after kids are in bed, on weekends."

"Fifteen minutes here, 10 minutes there," said my writing friend Melanie, a novelist and mom of two whom I met through a church writing group I organize.

People also wonder where I get my story ideas.

From everyday moments. While doing dishes or grocery shopping; during meals and carpools. Listening to kid conversations and musings. From walks to the park and road trips.

From life. It really goes back to the question, "When do you write?" to which I sometimes reply, "I am always writing."

I write while eating dinner with my family, soaking up the laughter of the children, the teasing, the taking too long to pass the salt which causes a battle to ensue; the early morning getting-lunches-packed sessions and the scrambling to find backpacks and matching socks; the individual moments I carve out with each child, whether it's walking to our local mom-and-pop bakery Sourdough Willy's for Sticky buns, fresh cookies and the best sourdough bread in the world; or on hikes in the woods listening to children as they find a new creature along the path. I ponder life during church sermons and sudsy dish rinsing sessions and tucking-in times at night, then write about it.

I am always writing. But my all-time favorite time to write? When my 4-year-old is sitting on my shoulders with his legs wrapped around my neck and his arms around my head; that is, as long as he is not throwing up.

Writing is a Lifelong Gift

"Without words, without writing, without books, there would be no history, there could be no concept of humanity." – Hermann Hesse

Sometimes I procrastinate on my articles due for the newspaper. I check e-mail, I clean my office, I make tea, I return phone calls, I start a load of laundry, anything to avoid writing. When I tell my husband this he says, "But you love writing," and of course, he's right.

Writing is my passion and it is what I do and it is an integral part of who I am. Yet, it is hard work. It is a difficult art. But, then somehow, I begin, and the muse hits me and the words and theme come together.

I've been a writer all of my life, having kept diaries since fifth grade. Without writing, it would be hard to remember some of the details of my childhood. Like the following funny diary entry, dated January 8, 1976 (age 11).

"Today was a pretty bad day for me. We had oatmeal for breakfast. It was two (sic) milky. At school I worked in the cafeteria. We went to gym in the morning. At school, in our class I am the president. We had 6 people missing. I had to lead the flag and do the lunch count. When I got home Mama was mad because we did not do the dishes. And she made a new rule that if you don't do your job you get 10 cents off your allowance. I get $1.00, Linda $1.00, and Martin 45 cents. Martin gets so much; when I was in 2ⁿᵈ grade I got 1 cent."

And this more sobering entry dated January 4, 1981 when I was 17-years-old: *"Around 6 p.m. the phone rang and Mama called me down and right way I knew who it was, Lynn Fischer. She was my best friend in fourth grade at Hosford. She remembered so much about our friendship; things we used to do, fights we used to get into, playing Queen Bee, chasing boys and making them get in trouble. Now Lynn is living in Yamhill, Oregon. Lynn just turned 17 and has a 1 ½ year old son named Ryan. She's married. What a total blow. We are in two different worlds."*

My children like to find out by reading my journals that I did watch TV after school during certain segments of my childhood, even though I had recalled differently. So much for using the logic that because I didn't watch TV after school while growing up, they shouldn't either. I wrote about the television shows SWAT, The Six Million Dollar Man, The Brady Bunch, and the Rich Little Show. They laugh at my past words about my siblings and my school and the allowance issues.

I have encouraged my children to keep journals as well. From the moment they could hold a pen, they have received journals to doodle in. When we go on family summer road trips, I bring journals for the kids; and each day I ask my kids to write about what we've done, places we've visited, people we've seen, thoughts they have. We purchase postcards and glue them in their journals. And, although sometimes they may at first grumble about having to write in their journals, later my children enjoy thumbing through them.

It's like appreciating Mozart, Van Gogh, and Charles Dickens. As we expose our children to the arts in various forms, they will hopefully grow to appreciate the disciplines, and adopt the aesthetic values as their own, and then pass them on to their children.

When our oldest son was 10, he said to me, "Mom, I don't need to know how to write; I'm going to be an engineer like Dad." My husband, a design engineer for over 20 years, pipes in: "Ryan, as an engineer, you need to know how to write. I write 30-page monthly reports at the first of each month."

And our daughter, who used to bemoan having to write, began keeping journals on her own when she turned 15. She continues to be an avid writer, and even wrote a Student Scope column for The Oregonian newspaper during high school.

When I encourage people to keep a journal, some say, "Oh, I'm not a writer," and I counter, "Everyone is a writer; we all have a story to tell." Sometimes when I ask if they will please help with the dishes or sweep the floor or vacuum, they will say, "Mom, I'm writing in my journal, or I'm reading," and they know I will not make them stop such valued activities.

As a mom, I try to write down things that my children say before I forget. On one family road trip to California in 2004, I had recorded questions my children were asking, like: "Do cows get hot? "Why are barns red?" and "Where do cobras live?" Brilliant musing.

And, writing, of course, not only records firsthand accounts of our story and history, but it also highlights the beauty of life. I think of the simple children's tale, *Frederick,* by Leo Lionni, where the field mice collect supplies for the long winter. All except Frederick.

While his fellow field mice gather nuts and straw and wheat, they ask him why he's not working; Frederick answers, "I am working, I am collecting sun rays for the cold winter days."

"And I'm collecting colors because the winter is gray."

"And I'm gathering words. There are many long winter days."

My kids are figuring me out. "Sometimes when I ask if they will please help with the dishes or sweep the floor or vacuum, they will say, "Mom, I'm writing in my journal," or "I'm reading," and they know I will not make them stop such valued activities.

Ode to Barns

I like barns. I especially enjoy old weathered barns, the ones you see on the loneliest of country roads, the forgotten ones, on the deserted back alleys of life, where the wheat waves in the hot dusty sunshine and the dry cornstalks sway in the wind; where old farm homes with wrap-around porches stand next to barns with the red paint showing signs of cracking and the white border turning faint creamy grey.

I do not remember exactly when this obsession began; I remember seeing old abandoned farms as a child, their sagging barns decorating the mountains of Austria on family vacations to visit *Omi,* my grandmother, who lived in Germany. I remember playing in barn hay lofts on lazy summer afternoons there, while chatting with other children and chasing chickens in the barnyard.

I often wonder why do I, a girl raised in the city, like barns so much. I tell my husband I want to move to the country and buy a farm with a barn on it, but the closest I have gotten so far is when my husband rented a 100-year-old historic octagonal barn owned by McMenamin's for the evening of my 40th birthday.

Although I cannot pinpoint exactly when I began delighting in barns, the inner yearning of what they represent is finding a voice in my life. Barns, with their flaky paint and wooden roof and old planks and creaky floors, beckon us to return to a simpler, unhurried lifestyle, where swallows and roosters and children and cows and kittens feel at home.

I love to see the tall tan grass in country pastures bending in the breeze, the wildflowers dotting the fields along the highways, the black and white cows grazing on the other side of worn white wooden fences, the sheep drinking at the creeks in the meadows, and the lonely barns every few miles. Barns represent a country life that is fading from many parts of our world.

Maybe it's their quietness, their calm colors, earth tones, shades that take me back to nature, colors close to the earth from which we were formed.

Barns somehow speak to the inner person, the artist within, the part that can get lost and forgotten and neglected and overlooked in the all-too-often rush of suburban family life.

When I am near barns I can breathe.

I like to take my children on drives to the country in search of old barns. We live in an area with several barns nearby, and I never tire of them. I point out barns to my children on journeys to the beach and on road trip vacations.

As I travel along country roads and gaze out my window, I ask my children to turn off their electronic equipment, their Walkman and Gameboys, and dare to discover. To notice. To appreciate. To take in the natural beauty that surrounds them.

And whenever I see anything that even comes close to a red wooden structure in the distance, I lift my voice in excitement and say to my children, "Hey, you guys, look ahead, there's a barn. Isn't that barn neat? Let's stop and get a photo."

Sometimes I ask my children to pose in front of barns so I can capture the moment. Children and barns go together; both possess innocence, simplicity, wonder. When we visit the parents of my childhood best friend in Corvallis, Oregon every year, I always take photographs of my children in front of their light green and white barn.

I desperately want my children to be just as enamored with barns as I am. That they would long to come to the country, as far or near as that might be, in search of barns and open spaces and wildflowers in fields. But right now, my first grade twin boys and my eighth grade son, to be sure, probably just want to play with their electronic toys.

But someday, when they are older, they may come to realize what barns represent. My daughter, at 15, already takes many photographs with her camera of seasides and sunsets and her brothers digging in the sand on the shore.

And of barns.

Maybe the rest of my children will only fully appreciate what barns mean as they thumb through their photo albums when they are older, and see photographs of their sweet smiling faces in front of the crusty wooden red or green structures.

Or when they drive by a familiar spot in the country and wonder what is missing, and notice that the scenery has changed.

And they will come to realize that what used to be a barn in the distance is now paved over with a highway or an office building or a busy subdivision.

And they will understand that it's true what I have said all these years, that they're selling the country; and my children will come to appreciate that their photographs and memories may be all that remains of barns.

And these words, my ode to barns and sunsets and wildflowers and meadows and creeks and children.

A Word is More than Just a Word

I was at church and my children wanted to join me for the "big church" service rather than go to their individual Sunday School classes. I so enjoy having my kids in church with me. It seems like so much of church is segregated. Preschool in one location, grade school elsewhere, junior high in one room while high school in still another spot. And singles somewhere else.

As we sat through the service, my children asked questions or bugged one another, just a little bit, and I had to remind them to be nice to one another; and sometimes I worried that they were distracting other people. I was encouraging them to worship and sing and look up passages from the Bible. June, who works at Thai Orchid restaurant where we often get take out, had asked to join us for church, and she brought her third grade daughter along.

After the service, I introduced June to various people, and as we were about to walk out of the sanctuary, a man I did not know came up to me and said hello. I thought he was just being friendly as people are in church. But then, what he said to me made an impact: "I saw you at different times throughout the church service, and I like the way you interact with your children."

I thought about it later, and continue to ponder that interaction. What a difference it made in my life. It somehow validated what I was doing as a mom with my children. And it reminded me of the importance of getting involved in people's lives. To take the time to encourage others, to build them up with words, to risk.

In many segments of American society, where everyone seems so independent, so self-sufficient, so "I don't want to bother you," it was refreshing to have a person that I did not know offer a specific observation about me. Especially because my kids were not "perfect" in service, and I had been concerned that they were distracting others.

I remember when I first started writing my "On the Home Front" family column for *The West Linn Tidings* in 1999, Bob Bigelow, the publisher of the newspaper, had said that he liked my writing, pointing out my third column, which was titled "Cherish the Treasures along the Road of Life." He then asked the receptionist if they were paying me to write my column. They were not. He said they need to be. And that is how I became a paid columnist, a dream come true. A year later, Bob Bigelow died unexpectedly of a heart attack at age 42.

Both of these gentlemen's words spoken to me over 10 years apart impacted my life. They gave grace and light and encouragement for the moment. And reminded me of the importance of daring to get involved, to affirm others, to talk to them, to build up one another, using words, which are more than words. Ephesians 4:29 in the New Testament comes to mind: "Let no unwholesome word proceed from your mouth, but only such a word as is good for building others up according to moment, so that it will give grace to those who hear."

On my daughter's tenth birthday, we went to get our hair cut together. The hairdresser's name was Candace, and she said something to me that stuck. "You have beautiful hair. So does your daughter. You should tell your daughter every day, that she has beautiful hair." I thought about my growing up years and how my mother used to say to me, "You have a beautiful face," and "You are very pretty." Those words have stayed with me.

Words go into a permanent tape recorder in your mind that you rewind. The vice principal at Cleveland High School in Portland, which I attended for four years, encouraged me after I did not do so well on my pre-SAT test scores. He said, "Tests don't measure everything. You have a lot else going for you. You are outgoing. You give back. You are involved in student government and music and sports. You are friendly to everyone." Those words were uttered more than half of my life ago, but I can still picture sitting in that vice principal's office and hearing his kind words.

I think of people in our lives that we know really well, how their words impact us that much more. And how our words make a difference in the lives of others.

Words. They are grace and prayers and light and beauty. And, they change lives. Spoken by people we've known for a long time, or those we've just met. And may never see again.

HOME

Home is where one starts from. – T.S. Eliot

The Dinner Hour

It's 5 p.m. and I'm scrambling to get dinner going. My husband Chris will be picking up our older kids from high school cross country practice while I'm indulging the three younger ones with Public Television.

I've known all day that I'm making dinner, something I do almost every evening, but it still feels rushed at about the same time; and while it's a struggle to make it happen, I know that this family ritual is worth the effort.

There is nothing like that feeling when all seven of us are finally assembled at the dining room table for dinner. After having been away from one another all day, at school and work and sports and appointments, even within the same house in separate rooms, it's sweet to come together, at home, corralled in one spot for the dinner hour.

I bring out my German porcelain, either the white with white roses, or the multi-flowered cream plates, and ask the kids to set the table. Seven plates and seven forks and knives and seven cups. And right now sunflowers from our garden brighten the table.

Two-year-old Augustin points to the table center piece vase, reminding me of how he helped pick yellow blossoms with his Dad and brothers: "Flowers for Mommy, flowers for Mommy."

My husband and my children love the smell of dinner cooking when they first walk into our home. On days when I'm not as prepared, I do the trick I learned from Focus on the Family: quickly sauté sliced onions and garlic in olive oil so they think there's something good cooking. That aroma means home.

"What are you making for dinner, Mom?" is often the first question I hear out of my kids' mouths when they meander in, backpacks and shoes shed at the door.

It's the same question I asked of my mom when I came home from school and sports. Dinner was of vital importance to me growing up. I especially savored my mom's Goulash and Rouladen (cabbage rolls) and Levanzen (yeast pancakes).

In today's busy world of soccer and music lessons and PTA meetings and late nights at the office and cable television and the internet, it's easy for families to forgo eating dinner together in favor of convenience. Fast food in the car seconds before soccer or micro-waved instant meals plopped in front of our kids who are on the internet while we dash off to check our e-mail.

40

The subject of family meals came up in last weekend's church service where Pastor Dale mentioned that one reason why the foundations of family life are floundering is that families don't sit down to eat together.

I confess, though, there are days when I haven't succeeded in making the world's best dinners, meals where I've merely opened a jar of spaghetti sauce and offered it on top of over-cooked pasta and a loaf of Sourdough Willy's bread, if we're lucky. And there are evenings when our meals should be called the *Dinner-15 minutes*, not the Dinner-Hour, but I still think that a small pocket of time gathered together is better than no time.

Just trying to figure out what to make for dinner each day at 4:30 in the afternoon is somehow huge, yet alone insisting on eating it together. The act of corralling all seven of us around the table takes dynamite sometimes.

I usually start with a warning: "It's almost time to eat," then "two more minutes, please wash your hands," then, "Wesley, please tell Rachel it's dinner time," and "Mickael-Josef, find Daddy and say, 'Dinner's ready.'"

If everyone's not at the table when my husband comes in, he smiles, "Augustin, please ring the cow bell," our clunky, *loud, real, cow* bell we bought at a farm supply shop in a village in Germany back in the olden days when we were able to go to Europe as a family, with "only" two children. The cow bell embarrasses the older kids. And me. And that gives my husband even more satisfaction when he rings it or has Augustin do the honors.

When we're finally seated at our oak rectangular table overlooking the creek in our backyard, we have a momentary quiet before our meal begins, a brief calm before the storm, when we pray and thank God for our food.

"Wesley's eyes are open," Mickael Josef reports. "Well how would you know if yours weren't open too?" Wesley counters. Then, "Ryan won't hold my hand," and "I'm not holding your dirty hands."

And I just sit there chuckling knowing that God must be smiling too, and it's all okay. We're all home.

As we say "Amen," the twins break into the chant, "Aaa-men. Aaa-men. AA-men, A-men, A-men. Again boom."

We begin passing the food and have only all been seated for a moment when our new grey kitten, Kujo, dashes between our feet and the rumble of the dinner hour gets started. Mickael Josef falls to the floor to try to catch Kujo, while Augustin cheers. Then Wesley dashes off somewhere.

"Where are you heading, Wesley?" I ask.

"To the bathroom," he announces skittering across the floor.

The phone rings, and Chris insists we ignore it, but Rachel has to check Caller ID in case it's related to the night's carpools. Good answer.

Augustin spills his juice while Wesley darts to the closet to get a towel to mop it up, and then Rachel disappears. "No cell phone," I insist.

"How was school today you guys?" I try to get conversation going.

That reminds Mickael Josef, as he runs for his backpack to show me his book.

"Please pass the bread, Wesley," Ryan says.

"Mom, Ryan didn't take any salad," Wesley tattles.

42

"Make sure you eat salad everyone," I insist.

Rachel is back and I ask how cross country was.

"Fine," she answers.

"Ryan, how are you doing in math?" Chris wonders.

"Okay."

"Who'd you sit by at lunch today, Micki and Wesley?" I wonder.

"Micki has a girlfriend," Wesley reports, adding, "actually two."

Giggles. Bright eyes. Laughter.

As we muddle through the dinner hour, with kids jumping up, dashing here and there, shot-gun answers to questions, the other noises begin, the ones produced by the male species in our family, the ones that cultivate chortling and snorting and hilarity at our dinner table.

It's a guy thing to be sure, and with just a hint of a chuckle from their Dad, they know they have permission to continue.

Sometimes as I listen and watch all the buzzing and clanking and crashing and humming and rumbling I savor the moment and tell myself, this is the stuff of a charmed family life. The things that people who are in the middle of disaster only dream about having.

Then other times I crave a quiet dinner at a local restaurant. Alone.

Then the kids compliment the meal with a "Good job, Mommy," something my husband constantly reminds our children to say to me.

When we're all gathered together at the dinner table, sharing a meal, we are home.

The Day the UPS Man Shows Up

It all happened the day the UPS man came to my door. I had been waiting for him. And what he was bringing is what my husband calls mud. Expensive mud.

I call it porcelain and china. Some people collect dolls, or jewelry, but my enduring collectible item is pretty tea-cups and saucers and teapots and plates and figurines. So, the reason for the UPS man is clear – to bring me a package of porcelain.

And, the moment he arrives happens to be a quiet moment. The twins are asleep. My older two are still at school.

Then, at the exact instant when I say good-bye to the UPS man and begin to open my package, my 2-year-old twins wake up. It's like they heard the rustling. They know how to climb out of their cribs, and so they join me as I'm admiring my new items and checking for damage and such.

They decide to do a little checking of their own. The large box that the china was delivered in, filled with little popcorn Styrofoam S's, will do just fine, thank-you very much.

I look over at them, and realize chaos is about to hit. All those little Styrofoam S's are about to be thrown all over my living room, a snowstorm of white Styrofoam S's if I don't stop the twins.

Then I see that big yellow school bus coming down the street, which means Chaos Part Two is coming.

I decide to let my two 2-year-olds unpack the countless little Styrofoam S's. I don't want to stop their creativity, I tell myself.

At first, they unpack them slowly; they keep glancing over at me as if to get my permission. They know they are about to make a mess, and I know they are about to make a mess. But I don't stop them as it will keep them occupied while I finish admiring my new plates and cups.

When the older kids come stomping up the stairs with neighborhood kids in tow, they are all ready for a snack. They shed their backpacks and shoes at the front entryway.

Then the twins get more bold with the Styrofoam S's, now unpacking them by the handfuls, and then armfuls, throwing them everywhere, laughing more and more with glee in their voices, until they decide to just turn the box over. They are giggling while saying "funny, funny." Styrofoam S's end up underneath chairs, all over my living room, beneath my sofa, and under the dining room table.

My older two children are chattering away and joining in the fun with the twins. They stop briefly to eat their snack while tossing school papers my way.

"Mom, read this."

"Mom, sign this."

"Mom, Ryan's not sharing."

"Mom, Rachel hit me."

I'm trying to relax in the middle of this chaos, while quickly putting away my new china. I recall the words which the woman working at West Linn City Hall said to me, when I was chasing my 2-year-olds around while getting my speeding ticket reduced. The twins were in this whirlwind of stimulus overdrive, with elevator buttons to push, drinking fountains from which to drink, stairs to run down. The woman must have seen the frazzled look on my face, while I tried hard to look composed. "You'll miss this time when they are grown. The time goes so fast," she said.

When the twins are throwing Styrofoam S's down the stairs, I want to stop them, but the phone is ringing, and then the overcooked fryer chicken on the stove top needs to be deboned. Then one of my twin boys accidentally hurts his brother, who comes crying to me, "Brother awwee. Brother awwee."

Then there is a knock at the door. This time, though, I hope it is not the UPS man.

My Dynamic Duo

Here it was just my twin 2-year-old boys and I on a Friday night, while my husband took our older two children skiing for the first time of the season.

I decided to take the boys for a walk to get pizza and a DVD. I figured if I let them walk instead of taking the stroller, they'd be exhausted come bed time which makes life easier for me.

While looking at the movies in the video store, one of my little ones decides he doesn't want to walk and begins to drag his legs instead. He goes completely limp and begins giggling. I warn him to stop, but it's too late. His twin brother caught on and the twin personality is well under way.

Here I am on a Friday night, trying gracefully to drag my limp twin 2-year-olds through the video store. I'm attempting to not make a scene. I am working on reasoning with two 2-year olds while smiling at all the people glaring at me. I say "Aufstehen," (which means 'Get up,' in German). I try to remain as calm as possible, but then my little ones laugh even more as the noise level rises.

So I do what every good parent does. I bribe them with the promise of candy. Works like Lucky Charms cereal. For a while. Until they see the big gum ball machine near the checkout stand. They both dart over there and they just can't contain themselves as their voices get louder with excitement, and I'm just thinking, get me out of here.

Life with twins. Three personalities wrapped up into two. By themselves they each have a personality, and then together they become a third person. One twin gets an idea to do something and begins doing it, and he may have stopped doing it had his brother not joined in the behavior as well.

Never a dull moment. Take another example. The twins moved our little fan away from our wood stove and took it into their bedroom, where they plugged it into an outlet and pretended to be blow drying their hair. Were they imitating me blow-drying my hair in the mornings? Who needs toys?

I remember just after the Christmas season thinking that their new Winnie-the-Pooh Duplos and their remote control backhoes would keep them busy for a long while; but that only lasted an hour. Then they were back to their favorite toys: plugging in vacuum cleaners, putting egg beaters into the key holes of our grandfather clock, taking their potty chairs to brother Ryan's book shelf to climb up and see what there is to play with in their big brother's room.

And just think of the double duty dynamic duo at dinner time at age two. One twin begins hitting his spoon on his high chair tray, then, as if he's a symphony conductor, he looks at his brother who, as if on cue, also starts pounding his spoon against his high chair tray, and they're laughing and giggling as it's getting louder and louder.

When I'm holding one twin, the other always wants up. If I buy them the same toy and they are each holding their own toy, they still want the other twin's toy, even though it is exactly the same size, color, model, make, and serial number.

At a couple of weeks old, when I first dared going out in public with them, people would say, "Double trouble."

But I'd say, "Twice as nice."

They're my dynamic duo.

Homework Never Ends

It is 10:30 p.m. on a recent weekday in September. While many adults in the "non-parenting" or "post-parenting" world are watching their favorite television show or curled up with a good book or possibly even already in dreamland, our seventh grader asks my husband, "Dad, can you check my math?"

I know my husband's tired and has to get up early for work the next day, but he says, "Sure.'

Other evenings, I hear, "Mom, will you take a look at my paper?" "Mom, can you sign here?"

I remember my daughter's first day of eighth grade; she came home and asked me "Mom, what's your definition of science?"

I wondered, "Shouldn't *you* be defining science?"

"No, my teacher wants us to ask our parents for their definition," she said, grinning.

Back to evenings filled with homework. Back to racking our brains trying to remember science and algebra and writing punctuation rules.

My husband helps with the math, telling the kids when they need to redo certain problems while I edit papers, place commas appropriately, and point out run-on sentences.

And sometimes helping with homework simply means reminding our children to find the information themselves in their books, or to check a paper on their own.

I talk to my friends with children, saying that when I was growing up, I do not remember asking my parents for homework help at 10:30 at night, or at any time for that matter. As a kid, I did homework alone. I consulted a friend or two maybe, but I mostly fended for myself.

My mom friends agree. They rarely asked their parents for help with homework either.

I mentioned it to my husband the other day and he laughs, "Yes, I thought I finished school in 1984 with my engineering degree, but instead I think I will be redoing school five times."

It is perhaps a different generation today with more being expected of parents. Statistics point to the fact that successful students have involved parents. I must say that I love being active in every part of my children's lives, and I am grateful that they ask me for homework help, and also that they want me to come to watch their school and church and sports activities. I enjoy supporting my kids, and being there for them.

They look for me in the audience at their band concerts and sports events. Their eyes scan the crowd searching for my reaffirming smile. They value my input. There has been so much joking about soccer moms, but I am here to say, Bravo to soccer moms. And band moms and cross country moms and youth group moms and homework helping moms. And dads.

Sometimes, though, at 10:30 at night, I must confess, I am tired and would like to be reading my own book at my bedside rather than trying to remember where a comma goes in my kids' homework assignment.

Home Base

At my twins' kindergarten T-Ball practice, a mom of another T-Baller asks me, "Whose mom are you?"

"I am Wesley and Micki's mom," I answer, and return the question, "Which little guy is yours?"

The exchange made me think about how being a mom is our identity. It is more than a job. It is who we are.

And it is the most important, most enchanting, sweetest, all encompassing part of who we will ever be.

When my "last" baby, whom my husband eagerly reminds me is "not a baby anymore," began saying "Mamma" for the first time, it was like the angels were speaking to me.

"Mam-ma" little Augustin says when he sees me, his eyes lighting up and his smile melting my heart, and he says it in his sweet little high pitched 13-month-old way. When he says

"Mam-ma" there is no other word in the world that matters at that moment.

Mama to a child means warmth, protection, nurturing, beauty, safety. It is everything good and pure and simple in the world to our child.

Being a mom is perhaps the single most important title I will have. Who I am as a mom matters for a lifetime. I remember how my older son, Ryan, who was a shy 12-year-old, introduced me to one of his new friends last year.

He said, "This is *My mom*," pointing to me and glancing at his pal. I had no name other than "*My mom*" and it was a perfect introduction.

As moms, we are our children's home front – their home base. I think of the game children play called, "Tag;" in that game, there is a home base, a place where participants cannot be tagged, a location where they are free to relax for a moment before running away from whoever is "It."

That is what moms are to their children. Home base.

When someone asks stay-at-home moms what they do for a job, they should never answer, "I don't work; I'm just a stay at home mom." Nor should they qualify what they do by adding, "But I used to be a counselor," or "I used to be a teacher," or "I used to be a nurse."

They should stop right there.

"I am a mom" is all that is needed.

Whatever job a mom had before, she is probably still all of those things. And more. Moms are just not getting a paycheck right now.

A mother's paycheck comes 30 years later when people ask her children, "What was your mom like?" and they answer:

"My mom was nice."

"She sacrificed for me."

"My mom made the best crepes on Saturday mornings."

"And always had cookies baking."

"My mom went to all my band concerts."

"My mom sat through my basketball games."

"And she made sure I finished my homework."

"My mom read to me."

"My mom prayed with me."

"My mom prayed for me."

"My mom tucked me in at night."

"My mom said 'I love you' to me all the time. And I felt it."

In the mean time, moms get little bonuses along the way.

Like last weekend when I came home from a mom's night away, the sweet sound of the pitter-patter of feet racing towards the door filled my ears.

It was my 6-year-old twins dashing towards me and falling frantically into my open arms, these sweet freckle-faced little front-teeth-missing boys with blonde buzz haircuts, whose innocent high-pitched voices exclaim my favorite word in the whole wide world, "Mommm-mmie! "Momm-mmmie!"

That is paycheck enough for me.

REAL-LIFE MOM ~
REAL FAMILY LIFE

Motherhood: All love begins and ends there.

— Robert Browning

On Flying Nativity Figures

We have this Nativity set made of carved olive wood, imported from Israel, that I purchased at a church bazaar when our now high school children were toddlers. It is a very simple set, with Joseph, Mary and baby Jesus plus the three wise men, shepherds and a couple of sheep, one now with only three legs, and a donkey with an ear clipped off.

But we adore that Nativity set. It represents real life. My husband built a stable for it, and every year while decorating our Christmas tree the children arrange the little wooden figures facing Jesus in the manger. My husband crafted a wooden barn-like structure in which to place our nativity set.

I am glad this Nativity set is wooden and not porcelain so my kids can play with the figures, but the other day my children gave new meaning to the phrase "action figures."

The scene went like this: While fixing dinner and listening to Christmas music, I looked over and saw my twin sons, 9, making the wise men wrestle and box one another along with Joseph and the shepherds, complete with sound effects. "Pow, wow, pow, pow!" And "uhh," when one fell.

Then the Magi and Joseph and shepherds were flying through the air as my youngest, Augustin, 3, giggled hysterically. Sheep were scattered on the couch and the donkey was in the kitchen and baby Jesus was nowhere to be found.

For a moment I wanted to stop all this, thinking these were sacred symbols and my boys should not be throwing them around. But then I decided not to interrupt their play. I realized they were just being boys enjoying the moment. They were not mocking anything.

So what if the manger scene is not perfectly arranged? Is that not the true nature of the Nativity story – and real life for that matter?

Just as that first Christmas in Bethlehem was probably not neat and tidy, our homes do not need to be like Martha Stewart's for the holidays. Though we do our best to create a festive place during this time of year, life and Christmas with kids will not always be perfectly organized and arranged. And that is perfectly okay.

We have a home that has life.

I think of our Christmas tree filled with all kinds of decorations, including handmade ornaments. We have no theme for our tree. Instead, every ornament is welcome, telling stories and bringing back memories.

One ornament is a frame made from Popsicle sticks with red and green and gold glitter that houses a photograph of my twins in preschool. While we decorated our tree, one twin, Wesley, sat holding this ornament, teary-eyed. When I asked him the reason for his melancholy, he said: "I wish I were little and cute again, like Augustin."

A perfectly themed Christmas tree would not bring about this kind of reaction in my children.

While I was growing up, I remember going often to the home of my friend Jeanie in Corvallis, Oregon. Her house was always warm, a place where everyone felt welcome, a down to earth spot where you did not worry about messing up the living room or bedroom. I did not feel that welcome in every friend's home I visited over the years, but I most definitely knew the difference between the two kinds of homes, from a very young age. I still love visiting Jeanie's family in Corvallis, and now I bring my family there as well.

As a mom, I want to create a home for my family and friends, both during the holidays and other times, that is welcoming and comfortable and easygoing and real. When Breezy – a friend of ours who was a member of the high school Bible study group that I led at church – stops by and I begin to apologize for my house not being in perfect condition, she reminds me of what I have always emphasized, that my home is not a museum. People live here.

I remember when a good friend of mine stopped by unexpectedly, my house looked something like this: Dishes were piled up in the sink and on the counter and on the table; Cheerios were scattered on the floor beneath the highchair, and the table was decorated with unread mail and lunch plates; tiny Lego's and building blocks were all over the carpet. Yes, I was stressed out.

I kept apologizing to my friend – she witnessed the uncensored version of my home life with five children - and she said, "You are fine and it is not about a perfect house and you are showing hospitality toward me."

No, I don't need a perfect house, but a home where my children can be themselves and relax and where there is time for one another.

I remember Augustin, when he was 3-years-old, asked me and everyone else about 50 times, "Mommy, can you play Candy Land with me?" which I did play even though I needed to straighten my house. (I remembered why my husband threw out our first Candy Land game that my older children had.)

And, when the twins were 9-years-old, they requested, "Mom, can you play Dragonology with us?" and I did, despite having work in front of me.

And when Ryan, 15, was reclining on the couch watching his twin brothers amusing themselves at Monopoly, I stopped myself from asking him to help me with dishes, letting him instead relax with his brothers.

And, I savor sipping tea with Rachel on our deck, despite having loads of unfinished housework to complete.

I want a home for our family that is a real, live, breathing space. A place, even, where wise men figures can sometimes be seen flying through the air.

Craving Quiet then
Ready to be the Ma-Mo

I felt lost as I watched the rest of my family, 1970's tent trailer in tow, drive down our street.

"Why was I not going with them for the first part of our Timothy Lake camping trip," I asked myself. Guilt came over me and a feeling of sadness over what I might be missing.

Yet, another part of me thought, "Wow, what a rare opportunity – home alone. Quiet and solitude."

The reason I was staying behind and driving up later to join the family was to work – writing my column and editing the weekly Style and Night on the Town magazines. Yet, even under the pressure of writing and editing deadlines, I was still looking forward to savoring extended moments of quiet.

As a family we have done many camping trips together, both near and as part of summer road trip vacations. I love experiencing hiking in the woods, taking long walks along pathways, sleeping in the tent trailer, roasting marshmallows at evening campfires, and looking at the stars at night on the lake with my children. There's a simplicity and beauty in watching my children delight in nature. It's always such an adventure.

I had never stayed behind while my husband took the kids overnight. But this time, as I knew I couldn't get my work done before we were to leave on Sunday, I said that I would come up a day later. My husband suggested that I make it two – work on the first day, relax on the second.

My friend Shelley who is a devoted mother of three understands my feelings: "I crave a day alone," she tells me.

My husband Chris and my mother-in-law chuckle teasingly when I say "I used to be a loner."

"Yeah, sure, you're a loner. You, who strike up conversations in public restrooms with people, a loner? Tell me another joke," my husband teases.

But it's true, I was a shy kid who liked being alone; I delighted in reading and writing and drawing and running. When I grew older, I became more outgoing. And yet, I still appreciate my time alone. Moments of solitude to think, to reflect, to write, to pray, to read poetry and Henry David Thoreau next to a trickling stream, near a patch of wildflowers. Thoreau deliberately boiled life down to its basics – nature, simplicity, basking in wooded solitude by Walden Pond. He revered the outdoors and quiet.

I'm absorbed in a world filled with the live music of five children, a husband and a sometimes frenzied, suburban family life where every moment is bombarded with commitments. My thoughts are interrupted and every ounce of my being is permeated with people coming and going. And I love every minute of it.

Yet, I admit, I find myself craving the solitude and quiet I once took for granted.

When I mention to my husband my desire for a moment of calm at home, he reminds me with a twinkle in his eyes, "You prayed for twins, you wanted a large family," and it's true; and I *love* my family and having a house full of kids. My kids' friends end up at our house because there is always something going on, which I so enjoy.

So many people say to me, "You have such a beautiful family, you are really blessed," and I know I am.

And, at the same time, I savor moments to myself, to regroup, rejuvenate, recharge. I long to listen to my music – to read and write – with the knowledge my mind won't get jumbled with chaos and clutter and being the judge and jury of kid arguments.

All that to say, I admit I did enjoy my two quiet nights home alone, and then I drove to join the family at Timothy Lake, bringing along tidings of Krispy Kreme donuts. When my children spotted my car, they dashed towards me. And as I climbed out of my vehicle, they all embraced me, and my youngest ones jumped into my arms and they said they missed me. And 2-year-old Augustin says, "Mami, Mami. You're the Ma-Mo," and I felt like the queen of the world.

Rejuvenated and rested, and now surrounded by my blessings, I was ready to be the Ma-Mo.

Crank up the Energy -
Here Come the Boys

Once I was picking up my twins, then 4, from church preschool, and I asked the teacher how they did in school that day.

"They were just okay," the teacher began, adding that she had to ask them to be quiet once or twice. Then, while I was still standing there, the teacher begins saying good-bye to another mom, who was holding her preschool girl, and the teacher says, "But this little girl, she was perfect – she sat quietly the whole time and said nothing."

The mother of the little girl seemed to understand more than the teacher, and offered, "Ahh, the difference between girls and boys."

Needless to say, I did not send my boys to that preschool again.

Years ago, a mom friend of mine shared with me a conversation she'd had with her 3-year-old son's preschool teacher.

"Your son might have attention deficit disorder and need to be medicated," the teacher said to my friend, who was a first time mother.

I emphatically reassured this mom friend that her active 3-year-old boy most likely does not have attention deficit disorder, but is simply a normal, inquisitive, active, curious, smart little boy. My son was friends with her son, and just as active. Years later, they are now both smart, creative, and yes, active young men who are doing well in school and extracurricular activities, sans taking medication for any disorders in their lives.

My son Ryan, when he was in fifth grade, did a research project on Thomas Edison, for Mrs. Cheri Weaver's Night of the Notable event at Cedaroak Park Primary School. The story of Edison went like this:

A 7-year-old boy named Thomas couldn't concentrate in the classroom at school. He got up often to go to the bathroom or to get a drink of water. He regularly asked the teacher to explain information being taught. The young lad could not complete simple instructions; he could not sit still and even stood up when doing assignments in class.

Frustrated with the boy, the teacher ordered him to sit down and listen. The other children in the classroom were quiet and said very little, and that suited the teacher just fine. The teacher labeled the boy "addled," which means "mentally confused" and "muddled," and when Thomas told his mother what his teacher said about him, she visited the school the next day asking for an explanation.

"Why did you belittle my son and call him 'addled'?" the mom demanded.

"He is always confused," the teacher said. "I think his brain is addled."

Thomas's mother knew that this, her seventh child, was different and she struggled with the way he rarely sat still. But she also realized he was bright and smart and inquisitive and full of energy and life. She watched him building things at home and working on projects for long periods of time.

Angry at the teacher's rigidity, Thomas's mom elected to home school her son. In time, he set up a laboratory to work on experiments. He went on to have his name associated with more than 1000 inventions – including the electric light bulb, the movie projector, the stock printer, the microphone, the telephone receiver.

I've heard it said, that by our generation's tendency to instantly label active boys, Edison and Albert Einstein would have been tagged as hyperactive instead of brilliant. The lack of appreciation by some for the sweet, innocent, curious energy of our boys disheartens me.

Too many children – especially boys – are being tagged at young ages as hyper-active, and quickly put on medication, such as Ritalin. Past stories have brought to light attention deficit disorder disasters, including parents being taken to court for deciding to not give their child Ritalin any more, which has been a common medication for boys with Attention Deficit Disorder.

Bottom line is we must believe in our children and network with other parents about how their children are doing and be our children's advocate, as Thomas Edison's mother was. Many children don't need medication – they need direction, flexibility, change in activities, diet adjustment, alteration in their learning environment, and discipline – or a laboratory.

Mom Guilt

I raised my voice at my twin 8-year-old boys today.

I call it "raising my voice" because I feel guilty about saying what it probably really was: yelling.

Of course, my boys hadn't listened when I told them once, twice, three times to stop squabbling with each other and to stop teasing their little brother, which happens often. It goes both ways. Younger siblings tease older siblings as well. It is what kids do. It is what I did with my siblings when we were growing up as well.

As a parent, though I realize it is natural for children to have arguments, sometimes it just gets on my nerves more than other times. And that is when I have the tendency to raise my voice.

This is not the first time I've raised my voice at my children, and it probably won't be the last, although each time I always say I am sorry and promise them and myself to not do it again, just as they promise to not fight or argue again. But this is real life and I'm a real mom and real moms make mistakes and feel guilty for many things.

Guilt shows its head in so many circumstances: When I go somewhere with one child, leaving another behind; when I spend time in my office and hear my kids asking, "What's for dinner?"; when my children say, "You work too much"; when I didn't attend an event my child was in because I had to be at the event of my other child; when I savor taking time to myself. Some moms deal with guilt better than others.

They get over it, knowing that they are doing the best they can and they are trying really hard and they let their kids know they love them despite their shortcomings.

My husband says I must enjoy feeling guilty because I do it all the time. I once missed one of my daughter's two District track races even though I intended to see both events. Since the meets usually run late, I waited until the last minute to arrive and didn't count on the meet starting 30 minutes early or a traffic accident stalling me.

The guilt for missing my daughter's first race was so over-powering that I told my daughter that I saw the last part of her race, which she won. The words just came out after she had asked me if I saw her race. I then prayed she'd win her next race. So I could actually see it. And to ease my guilt.

She did win the second race and so I confessed about missing the first one. She was fine with it.

Even the best moms cannot attend every performance of their children's. I saw one of Rachel's longtime friends at that same District track meet, and she mentioned that her mom couldn't make it to watch her. Her mom is one of the most supportive, devoted, amazing mothers with five confident children, and she couldn't get to the District meet to watch her daughter.

Another weekend when my daughter wanted to have some alone time with me, one of her younger brothers asked to tag along.

"We're just doing girl things," Rachel said, eyeballing me that I better not give in.

But two blinks later, her brother was in the car. After a tennis match of words, he ran back into the house upset that he couldn't join us. I insisted on keeping it as planned, just a mom-daughter outing, but I still felt badly that my son, Rachel's brother, was hurt.

I would've felt guilty either way. Sometimes moms can't win.

Recently one of the twins announced, "Mommy's on her computer again. It's like Game Boy to her." Guilt. I should have been cooking or cleaning or helping with reading homework. But I also have work deadlines. Moms feel guilty for working.

In the movie "Cheaper by the Dozen 2," one of the grown kids in the film noted: "As Dad said, 'There are no perfect parents, but there are a million ways to be a good one.'"

Roller Coaster Parenting

I bought the 1989 movie Parenthood with Steve Martin for my husband for Father's Day, and we watched it the other night with the children. We had first seen the movie back in 1990 when our daughter was an only child. In 2004, three boys later, we are watching it again.

What my husband remembered about that movie when we watched it many years ago, is how it captures the real life emotions of parenting. The worries, the feelings, the chaos, the responsibility, the hurt, the joy, the laughter, the agony, the beauty, the heartache.

At the beginning of the film, they show a flashback of Steve Martin, the main "dad" character in the film, as a child when his father dropped him off at a ball game on his birthday to watch the game with the usher, whom the father paid to sit with his kid. The experience haunted the father character which Steve played.

73

The flashback in the film gives the context for why Steve Martin is trying so hard to give his three children a meaningful, happy childhood. The film forwards to today, where the dad character and his family are leaving a baseball game, hauling their chair pads and the overly priced souvenirs and the blankets and the bags and the sticky cotton candy; and the dad is carrying a sleeping child and one of the kids has to go to the bathroom. And once they are finally in the car exhausted, one of the boys sings the silly song, "diarrhea" over and over again, while the mom and dad try to drown out the noise. As a parent, you laugh to yourself and think, "I can relate."

You feel the chaos, yet there is beauty in the craziness as well.

Later in the film, they show Steve Martin trying to advance his career to support his family, and he is worried about his oldest son, age 10, whom the school suggests needs therapy, and he and his wife argue about child rearing issues.

The movie focuses on other parents as well, relatives of Steve Martin, dealing with their own sets of struggles with raising children. Throughout the movie, you see parents planning birthday parties and coaching Little League Baseball and worrying about their parenting styles and one of the sets of parents is preparing their preschool daughter for college. You view uncertainties and heartaches and joys – in other words, real life parenting with its ups and downs.

The film even shows parenting never ends, even when children leave the nest.

As a parent, you worry if you have given kids adequate training in life skills. You question parenting decisions. You

74

wonder if your discipline style is too rigid or too soft. You ask yourself if you have done enough to help your child make good friends. You are concerned whether you have been a good role model. You hope and pray you have taught them to be kind and to love God and others. You want to create a loving home for your family.

Yet parenting is hard and frustrating and emotionally draining and time consuming and selfless and difficult and it drives you crazy sometimes but you love it all the same.

Some things are just not covered in our parenting books. You learn by taking each circumstance individually, networking with other parents, using your God-given instincts, reading the Bible and praying a whole lot.

Once I told a friend how I was struggling. My husband was out of town and I had one of my twin babies crying, and I was trying to help my two school-age kids with homework while attempting to get the twins to bed. My house was a mess, and I said, "I have been having a hard time lately," and the friend said to me, "Oh, it's not that bad."

Reality is, though, that it is sometimes that bad. And it is okay to admit that we are having a hard time.

I hear my friends, who have two children, talk about how they struggle as well, how they are scrambling to keep the house picked up and to help their children with school and to figure out what's for dinner and to get their children to basketball practice and to arrange the carpool to play rehearsals and to be sure they make it to youth group church on time.

I saw an article in a women's magazine featuring a mom of nine children, who won some "Best Mom" c

Her kids all have perfect clothes on, and the mom was beautiful and in shape, and all the toys were picked up, and she had these built-in lockers for the children's items for when they walked in the door from school. And when her husband returned home from work this Best Mom had a home-cooked, five-course meal waiting for him on the elegantly set dinner table for eleven, along with a kiss at the door, and I thought, that is not my 5:30 p.m. reality.

When my husband walks in the door after work, here is what the scene sometimes looks like: I have just opened a jar of Spaghetti sauce and tossed some Angel Hair with it; and the baker's kids are delivering a loaf of sourdough I had requested; and the kids' backpacks and shoes and papers from school are scattered in the entryway along with my son's trombone.

And the fort the twins built is still in the middle of the living room, and the rattles and books are scattered over the carpet and graham crackers are strewn on the linoleum from lunch.

And my husband tells me work is hard and I had been frustrated with some school issues and the kids had been arguing.

In the middle of the movie "Parenthood," the grandma shares a metaphor for life about her experience on a roller coaster ride: "Up, down, up, down. Oh! What a ride. You know it was just so interesting to me that a ride could make me so frightened, so scared, so sick, so excited, and so thrilled all together. Some didn't like it. They went on the merry-go-round. That just goes around. Nothing. I like the roller coaster. You get more out of it."

76

Steve Martin's character dismisses the grandma's story, but his wife recognizes its wisdom reflecting the reality of both the struggles and joys – the ultimate adventure – and the roller coaster ride that parenting can be.

DELIBERATE PARENTING

These commandments that I give you today are to be upon your hearts. Impress them on your children. Talk about them when you sit at home and when you walk along the road, when you lie down and when you get up.

- Deuteronomy 6:6-9

A Letter from Prison

"Dear Mom, Thank you for writing me back. I love the picture and I'm hoping for more. I enjoyed our visit too, it was great to see you. It really reminds me of how much you and your family were always there for me. That's God's Love, what keeps me moving. I'm so blessed and thankful to have met you and your whole family. At least I know I still have family in Oregon. I love you guys and I miss you as well. I can't wait to see you again. Tell Chris I said hi and I miss him too. He and your family have introduced me to a whole new world I would never have known. Making apple cider and how to say grace in German. I remember when I came over you'd tell everyone to read your Bible and say your prayers, and that's exactly what I've been doing. I'm grateful. I still have hope for heaven.....I hope to see you some more. Thank you for coming to see me in jail. Thank you for everything you have done to and for me and my family. –Love, Jima"

Those are the words written to me by our 17-year-old Sudan refugee friend who is in juvenile detention. When Jima was 15, he began taking the bus from North Portland to our suburban house to stay with us on weekends. Jima joined us almost every weekend for a while. We met Jima and his family through a church outreach in 2006 and continued to stay in touch.

He came to church with us and we had tea and bagels afterwards, and we prayed before meals. Jima attended Bible study with my two older children Rachel and Ryan on Saturday nights at the Kings and the Hollands houses that the kids organized on their own.

Jima would be with our family when we made apple cider in the fall, he'd come camping with us in the summer, and he'd celebrate holidays with us. He did homeless outreaches we organized and he attended family gatherings. When I would tuck my children in at night, I'd always remind him as well to "Read Your Bible Say Your Prayers."

The rest of Jima's family of nine are also our friends. They have come over for Christmas and Easter celebrations. Tifisu, the mother, had never felt sand beneath her feet while running along the ocean before she and her children joined our family at the beach. The children adventured with us to Mount Adams Wilderness area where we hiked on the Sleeping Beauty Trail to reach the top with its amazing view.

Our church joined us in helping them and also assisting at sports camps in their neighborhoods, where we'd bring basketballs and baseballs and soccer balls, inviting any children in the neighborhood to join us.

But, after a while, turmoil and chaos set in for this family of nine, and Jima stopped coming to our home. And, when his 14-year-old brother Wang was shot by gang members in North Portland in early 2010, everything changed. The family needed to move far away, to escape the dangerous circumstances that surrounded them. But before they could move, the 14-year-old needed to heal.

The State asked if he could stay with us. We were thankful to be able to take this boy, a freshman in high school, into our home to live with our family. For seven and a half weeks.

What I began to realize right at the beginning of Wang's stay with us was the importance of being deliberate with children. Being intentional parents. I knew we had only a short window of time to make a difference in Wang's life as he became part of our family, and I wanted the time to count. To be memorable. I wanted Wang to experience a family life of togetherness, of caring, of sharing meals at the dinner table, of going on adventures, of attending church together, of family movie nights, of doing chores together and being accountable to complete homework and housework, of being part of a family.

One tradition that has been important to me is reading the Bible together at the dinner table. My husband and I have attempted to do this at various times on a regular basis, and sometimes it just did not get very far with active boys and a busy schedule. Though we always pray before meals, we were not as consistent to read Bible at the dinner table as a family. When Wang joined our family, God laid it on our hearts to be sure to remember to do this more regularly once again.

We also began reading the book called *Crazy Love* by Francis Chan out loud at the dinner table. The book focuses on getting back to the basics of falling in love with God and His word. Wang got really excited about the book and about following Christ, and he began reading the book on his own.

Wang was learning other truths while living with us. Once he had asked my husband to take him to school on his way to work. Up to that point, Wang had been taking the school bus. My husband told Wang that he would be glad to give him a ride, and that he needed to be upstairs at 6:45 in the morning.

The next morning when Wang had wanted a ride to school with my husband, Wang came into the kitchen at 7 a.m. and asked me, "Is Chris up yet?" I said, "Yes, Chris leaves for work between 6:45 and 6:50." Wang learned that my husband does not sleep in, but instead goes to work day in and day out to provide for his family. And Wang also learned the importance of commitment and following through on what you say you are going to do.

Wang also saw flexibility and grace demonstrated toward him. My husband had indeed left for work that day, yet knowing that Wang wanted a ride to school but wasn't upstairs on time, Chris only drove around the block, then came in through the front door, asking "Wang, are you ready?"

During Wang's seven week stay with us, we were deliberate about other things as well, such as having people over for fellowship; and I asked an African American friend of ours, Gerry, to mentor Wang while Wang stayed with us.

After the seven and a half weeks in our home, Wang's injuries were healed, and he needed to return to his family as they were moving out of state. It was a safety issue as the gangs were still after Wang. I wrote each of the children personal letters, and I wept as I wrote recalling memories we have shared the past three and a half years. I added photographs to each letter, photographs of us together at various adventures. I hope and pray they never forget.

The words in the letter Jima wrote to me from prison carve out a soft spot in my heart. He calls me Mom. And, he remembers how we said grace in German, and how I remind my children to, "Read your Bible and say your prayers."

Those are a few of the things I am intentional about emphasizing as a parent. I am also deliberate about going on adventures with my children and carving out individual time with each child. I make sure I ask our children questions about what they are hearing at school and church, and that we talk about God in real life circumstances. I like to look for the lesson in situations and movies and music, and speak to my kids about culture. I am intentional about telling my kids I love them, and about talking about forgiveness and flexibility and kindness and manners and relationships. I am deliberate about teaching my children to live by the word of God and to love their family and to follow Christ all the days of their lives.

Bottom line: I want to always remind my kids to live life to its fullest.

Reminding Kids to Mind their P's and Q's

When our oldest son was a freshman in high school, he was still a bit shy. When a pal from Boy Scouts called to remind him of an upcoming event, all I heard my son say upon hanging up was "Bye."

I emphasized afterward: "When someone calls to tell you something, you need to say, 'Thanks for calling.'"

When I mentioned "bashfulness" as the reason a mom gave for her 10-year-old daughter's impoliteness, my friend Kristi said, "Shyness is no excuse for rudeness."

As a parent, intentional etiquette training – such as the importance of an RSVP, making eye contact, showing gratitude, holding doors, writing thank-you notes, admitting fault, and the modern one of being careful of texting while watching movies or having lunch with a friend – seems missing in the priorities of busy parents.

Sometimes I wonder if some parents want to be their kid's best friend while forgetting the value of instruction. And sometimes children do just forget.

With family time spent in a car or in front of computer screens, kids don't learn to be mindful of others as they should. And parents can be part of the reason. Two incidents illustrated this for me:

While at Lake Merwin in Washington State one summer, we noticed a dog doing a number near us, and we assumed the owners, a mom and son, would pick up after their pet; but instead they walked away.

"Excuse me, I think you forgot something," my friend Michele said. "Mind your own business," the woman jeered, and her son, about 10, cursed us as they stormed off toward their car.

And while at my high school kids' district cross country competition one year, the leader of the boys' race hollered "watch out" at two grade school girls who were on the boys' race course. "How dare that high school guy treat our girls like that," the mother of the two girls complained to her husband.

He countered: "Our daughters were in the way, and we need to be careful."

His wife missed the point and insisted, "That runner had no right to yell at our girls."

While both of these moms that I observed had the opportunity to teach their kids respect for others during a particular circumstance, they instead missed the point, modeling the attitude that the world revolves around them, and I'll do what I please. I remember a friend of my son's coming over to watch a movie with us on one of our family movie and pizza nights, and this friend of my son's texted on his cell phone during the entire movie. Click. Neon lights. Click, click, click.

Parents need to emphasize to both older and younger children various etiquette concerns, and teaching as young as possible is optimal. Children learn.

When my youngest son Augustin was 2-years-old, he used to say to me, "Can you please get me some water, Mommy?" and "Thank you for the cookie, Rachel."

When we're in the van and someone lets us into traffic, my kids know to wave in gratitude; and there is no greater compliment than to hear parents of my kids' friends say, "Your children are always so polite." We constantly remind them to be verbal about their thankfulness.

I am well aware when parents have emphasized the value of manners to their children. Those are the kids I especially like my kids to invite into our home. They say thank you when I serve them dinner or drop them off at their home. They ask before taking seconds when eating with us.

As parents, it's our hope that "minding their p's and q's" becomes second nature for our kids. But it takes more than hoping. It takes specifically training and emphasizing and modeling good behavior.

A couple of months after I had talked to my son Ryan about etiquette while he is speaking on the telephone, I noticed him say, "Thanks for calling," when he hung up the phone.

"Ryan, how'd you learn to be so polite?" I ask smiling.

He answers, grinning, "From you, Mom."

It's Called the Off Button

When we arrived at our friend Carol Ann's home for a New Year's Eve party one year, I asked our hostess if we could limit the electronics for the boys. I wanted to interact with the kids and play board games with them, and I just cannot compete with neon lights.

Carol Ann's answer surprised me. "No worries — we don't have electronics in the house," she said. She is a mom of four girls, but with her nephew living with her now, I figured electronics were a part of their home life.

I admired my friend. Somehow, in our home, electronics seem to dominate our boys' interests. It seems addictive. I see the boys' behavior change after they have played on electronic toys too long — the boys become wired and tend to squabble more, and creativity just gets thrown out the window, as some studies have confirmed.

I must confess, though, that as a mom it is easier to let the boys stay plugged in longer than I know I should allow. It keeps them quiet downstairs and allows me to get a few things done upstairs. Sure they may squabble, but at least it is not in my presence. Afterward, though, I regret it when I see the intensity in their demeanor.

When my twins were 9-years-old they were at their friend Daryl's house whose parents had "grounded him from all screens," and I thought, kudos to his mom, Liz, for having the discipline to take away electronics. That same day, when my daughter was 17-years-old, she said to me, "Mom, I want to take the twins' DS's and X-Box and Game Boys away; they are getting way too addicted. Let's hide them until Christmas. And I will not give in like you always do." She could be the next Super Nanny on the reality TV show.

I always talk about the importance of kids playing outside and parents being strong enough to insist kids turn off their electronics. Let's see how long I last. My daughter though grins at me and says, "Mom, I am not giving in."

Indeed, I have found that banning electronics is one of the best disciplinary tools to use with the boys because it gets at something they care about. Call it tough love.

A few years later, we began a tradition of making Sunday an electronics-free day. After church, we typically get bagels and cream cheese for lunch, and after we eat together, we find a favorite spot on the couch to read or take a nap by the window. I look forward to that day. A day that God created for rest. Kids need to see parents using the off button as well.

The year that my daughter encouraged the electronics ban when the twins were 9-years-old was close to the Christmas season, and my twins decided to sew pillows as gifts for family members and for their secret Santas at school. Their enthusiasm was so sweet; at one point Wesley said he was going to make 12 pillows. I think in the end he made five.

Sans electronics, the boys also played more board games — and we joined them. They met neighbor kids at the park, amused themselves on the piano and read books for school. And my husband and I began thinking of gifts we could give them for Christmas that would continue to encourage non-electronic forms of entertainment, something definitely contrary to consumer buying predictions for the rest of America. Lego's came to mind. The boys had set aside their Lego's fascination due to their obsession with everything electronic, so we decided to try to re-spark that interest.

We got them looking up Lego sets online and in the Lego catalog, and that was all it took. They decided on a 1,326-piece "Star Wars" ship to top their wish lists.

The twins were thrilled to open that large package on Christmas morning. When it was time to go to Grandma and Grandpa's for Christmas dinner, they packed up their unfinished creations to continue working there, and we had to pull them away so they would eat dinner.

Finally, after a good 12 hours, they announced it was finished. When I said, "Hey, I am so proud of you two for putting together a 1,300-piece Lego ship," they corrected me. "Mom, it was 13 hundred and 26 pieces," they said, beaming. I stood corrected.

Things They'll Remember

When my daughter was in middle school and I asked her what advice she has remembered me giving her so far in her life, "Brush your teeth," is the first thing that came out of her mouth, which made her and her friend laugh. I encouraged more and she went on to say, "Get A's rather than B's."

So much for deep messages that I thought I was sending to my first child.

I believe now that she is 20, she would mention other things that I have emphasized in life, but this was through the eyes of a 12-year-old. It reminded me of the importance of pointing out things to our children that we want them to remember.

I asked my cousin-in-law what advice she remembers her mother giving her, and she said, "Never give up. Always complete a project."

I thought about what counsel sticks out from my upbringing.

"Get your college degree before getting married," my parents always said. Other words shared with us in various circumstances: Be the best at anything you do. Don't be mediocre. Value yourself in relationships, don't be too easy, and that meant for my sister and me to never call a guy. I mean *never*. My mom made it clear the guy should always call the girl on the telephone. I took that advice to the extreme: When I was engaged to be married to my husband, he said to me, "You can call me now."

Now as a parent I ask myself, what do I want to be remembered for? What advice do I want my kids to remember when they think back on their childhoods with me? My list would be something like this:

Yes, brush your teeth (actually I say "Brush, floss, brush").

Read your Bible.

Pray.

Ask God to show you His will for you. Then listen.

Don't settle for a mediocre life.

Help others.

Be compassionate and flexible.

Love God.

Be patient.

Forgive.

Family is the most important thing and all you will have, as friends may come and go.

Be good to your siblings. And to your Mom and Dad.

Your children are your legacy.

Be loyal.

Be a good friend.

Be kind.

Be real.

Don't talk badly about others.

Reach for your dreams.

Take the narrow road.

Play music, create art, sing, dance, love, be fun.

Go on adventures.

Walk, hike, bike, run.

Write. Draw. Read.

Never ever ever give up hope.

We are Our Children's Living Textbook

My friend Bea's 8-year-old daughter asked her one day, "Did you go to school to be a Mom?" "No, I learned how to be a Mom from my Mom," Bea answered.

"Well, where did she learn how to be a Mom?" the second grader continued. "She learned it from her Mom," Bea said.

"So, I'm going to learn how to be a Mom from you?" the 8-year-old deduced.

"Yes, well, I guess so," Bea said, chuckling.

Our children are watching us. And listening to us. And drinking in the world which surrounds them, the very fragrance of our being. The good, the human, and the *I wish I could erase what I just said* side.

Children will become versed in everything Mom and Dad. Our attitudes about people and God and work and church and social issues and modern society and giving and politics and life. Our time priorities, what we read, how much we give to others, how we handle stress and joy and money and decisions and annoying neighbors and driving during rush hour traffic.

Parents are role models for what is essential in life and that impacts children. My college friend Nancy said that she remembers her dad reading God's word daily during morning quiet times. Now Nancy treasures God's word in her life, and she is passing that value onto her children. And, Meri, another college friend, speaks so highly of the way her parents' prioritized family and continue to do so to this day as grandparents of Meri's children.

Kids will feel our love for them by the way we nurture and protect them and spend time with them during the day and at meals and at bedtimes; and they will absorb all of the words we say to them. Or don't say.

Children are like young apprentices, following us on the job, soaking up everything we are, training to eventually be a parent. I often wonder what things will come to mind as my children reflect on everyday life in our household.

Was I patient and kind and loving? Was I a good mom? What was life like at home? We should ask our children, as my friend Diane did when her children were young, "Are you having a happy childhood?"

Being a parent covers so many areas of life. Physical needs, emotional needs, spiritual needs, and social needs. Instilling values and teaching etiquette.

While I was growing up, working hard was an important value in my family. My parents started their marriage as immigrants from Germany; my mom had just graduated from college and my dad was still working on various degrees. They had about a dollar and a half in their pockets and a lot of discipline and determination to make it. My dad eventually earned his Ph.D. and became a well-loved professor at the University of Portland, while my mother was a teacher, stock broker, real estate professional, and stay-at-home-mom.

My sister, brother and I learned the value of work because we were required to work around the house; we did the dishes, we swept the floor, we watered the garden, we set the table, we cleaned the bathroom. Now, as a parent myself, I try to give my children the opportunity to labor both within the home and outside; in a family of seven, everyone's skills are needed.

My Mom collected coupons, always looking for ways to save money, and to this day she has coupons from the 1980's that she just cannot throw away. Sometimes she had so many coupons for so few items, that in the end it seems like stores paid *her* to shop. And here I am as a mother, clipping coupons, albeit not as faithfully as she did, but still always seeking out bargains.

My folks gave me a sense of adventure. Every few years while I was growing up we traveled to Germany to visit family and see the sites. I know it was a financial sacrifice, and our Christmases were never elaborate, but I'm grateful for the gift of travel. Today, my husband and I enjoy exploring the world with our children, going on day trips as well as longer road trip vacations.

So many other things that my mother did, such as cooking from scratch and making sure we had meals together around our dining room table, I now do for my children. Preparing crepes topped with lemon and powdered sugar was a favorite of mine growing up that I now make for my kids. We usually had meals together at the table as a family which is so important in connecting with your children.

Our parents took us to the opera and symphony at least once a year, and, though at times it was not my first choice of activity, I appreciated it once I was there. My childhood experiences instilled in me a love for the arts and music and literature, and now my husband and I make the arts a priority in our family.

And Mama and Daddy walked and bicycled to places in their Hawthorne neighborhood in Portland to pick up bread or milk, and they sent us plenty of times alone as well. I can remember riding my bicycle with a dollar in my pocket to the local gas station for a gallon of 99 cents milk or purchasing a dozen eggs on sale at Safeway, limit one, so all of the kids got to go, individually. I bet the grocery clerk knew our secret. And my husband's parents spent a lot of time with him and his siblings, enjoying family life. Chris speaks of hunting and fishing with his father and his family camped together and went on road trips and enjoyed the outdoors and shared family dinners on Sunday Nights.

Now, flash forward 30 years, and you see my husband and me making an effort to walk with our children in the neighborhood, to buy a gallon of milk or get a pizza for dinner. And we take our children camping and hiking and skiing and bicycle riding, and we go on road trips with my husband's parents' 1970s tent trailer. And we have family meal and movie nights each week.

And Chris takes the boys hunting with his father. And, I love how our youngest child, age 7, follows my husband into the backyard to plant a garden and water plants and pick a bouquet of flowers for me. Chris is so good about including the children in what he does around our home.

Of course, we look back on our childhood and are conscious of things we did not like about growing up, parenting patterns that we do not want to repeat with our own children. I remember my mom mentioning attitudes in her folks which she did not want to emulate, such as when her parents would say, "Because I told you so" after she asked them "Why?"

She also said that her parents sometimes wouldn't admit when they were at fault, while my Mom, who loved her parents deeply, felt it important to say, "I'm sorry." I do as well.

Being a parent encompasses so much more than only what you do. It's who you are towards your children and toward others. Your attitude, your patience and kindness and flexibility and sense of love and belonging you bestow on your children – things that are hard to define.

We need to be deliberate about parenting. What kind of Mom or Dad will we be? Or not be. How do we want to be remembered? Uptight or easy-going? Inflexible or patient? Uncompromising or forgiving? I want to make Christ the center of our lives, and read God's word together as a family. And serve those less fortunate. And pray with our children and talk to them about seeking God's will for their lives.

As parents we are our children's living textbook on parenting. May we write it well.

FROM THE MOUTH OF BABES

Questions About Angels

Of all the questions you might want to ask
about angels, the only one you ever hear
is how many can dance on the head of a pin.

No curiosity about how they pass the eternal time
besides circling the Throne chanting in Latin
or delivering a crust of bread to a hermit on earth
or guiding a boy and girl across a rickety wooden bridge.

Do they fly through God's body and come out singing?
Do they swing like children from the hinges of the spirit
world saying their names backwards and forwards?
Do they sit alone in little gardens changing colors?

- Billy Collins

Did the Devil Make Your Hands Hurt?

So my 7-year-old Augustin says to me last night, as he sees the psoriasis on my hands, "Mom, did the devil make your hands hurt?"

I was a bit distracted at the moment but then my husband said, "Cornelia, he's asking you a question." Augustin asks again, and then explains his question, "'Cause you said the devil hurts you and God makes good things happen."

I don't even recall specifically saying much about the devil to my son. Don't you just love the thoughts and questions of the mouths of babes? He didn't stop there. "Mom, I don't get why God just doesn't go down to hell and kill the devil."

Wow, the questions that come out of the mouth of my first grader. I encourage the questions and I also tell my children that I am not always able to find the answers in a quick, easy, one sentence statement. But I will always try to help him search Scripture and seek the wisdom of others.

Augustin is really asking the age–old question, one that some people say keeps them from following God. You'll hear people comment, "How can a good God allow evil in the world?" and "How can you say God is good when there is so much suffering in the world?"

It is tough to think about. As I read various passages in the Bible, I even see men and women of faith expressing doubts about God's goodness. I think of the reality of God giving us freewill and the existence of evil forces. But, sometimes the questions are still there. I am reminded of King David, who was considered a man after God's own heart, and yet he cried out to God: "My God, my God, why have you forsaken me?...O my God, I cry by day, but You do not answer; And by night, but I have no rest." (Psalm 22:1-2)

And, I love how David turns it around to show his trust in God, speaking truth into the situation. He says in the next verse: "Yet, You are holy. O You who are enthroned upon the praises of Israel..."

Ultimately, this question of Satan comes down to the reality of where our struggle has its roots. As we studied Ephesians 6 in my discipleship group with Linda Ebel, we are reminded that our struggle is not against flesh and blood, but against the powers, against the forces of darkness, against the spiritual forces of wickedness... (v. 12).

Why doesn't God just destroy the devil now? And does Satan cause my hands to be bad? Good questions and all I can say is, we are in a world that is not perfect and we are not perfect, and that is what makes life interesting. And, that is part of our life story which has ups and downs. One day, as it tells us in the Bible, the devil will be destroyed and one day my hands will be perfect.

But not today. And that is okay. Because it makes me trust God today, and it makes me depend on Him today, and it draws me to my knees. And, I pray that my children, too, will always be drawn to their knees, no matter what the circumstances are in their lives. That they would acknowledge our ultimate and complete dependence upon God. And that they would not be afraid of the questions.

Who Do You Love the Most?

When one of our twin boys was 5-years-old, he says to me, "Do you still love me?"

I am of course surprised by his question. "Yes, of course, I love you so very much."

"But Baby Augustin is so cute. Don't you love him the most?" he wonders.

I gather up my darling, sweet freckle-faced 5-year-old and say to him, "I will always love you, you are special to me. I have so much love in my heart for each of my children. And now we have another little baby to love, we are so blessed, and you are a wonderful big brother to him."

My 5-year-old's face lit up.

Children needing reassurance of their parents' love often becomes more pronounced when a new baby enters a family. And, with twins there is an ongoing comparison being made with one another anyway. A year after the first twin's question regarding whether I still love him, the other twin asks, "Who do you love the best?"

I answer, as I always do, "I love you the same, equally, totally, completely, one thousand percent each," as I wrap my arms around him, looking into his sky blue eyes.

In the mornings when I get home from my workout, I am greeted by my twins' high pitched voices announcing, "Mommy! Mommy!" as they race down the steps to see me.

One twin jumps into my arms and says, "I got her first. She's only my Mommy."

"I am both of your Mommies," I quickly correct, reaching around to embrace both of these little buzz-cut blonde then-6-year-old-bundles-of-all-boy.

What is it with children, and maybe especially twins, having to be loved "the most" and "the best" and "the only," as if somehow there is a shortage of a mother's love to go around?

I try not to encourage unhealthy competition amongst our children, such as saying, "Well, your brother does that so well. Maybe you could be like him," or "He got an A on his test, what happened to you?" Instead I try to find things that each of my children is good at and point that out.

Children need to hear that they are unique, that you love them for who they are, exactly as they are, right now, at this very moment. They need to feel that total, unconditional, flat out, my-mom-is-crazy-about-me kind of love.

From the moment that pink or blue bundle of joy is handed into the waiting arms of new parents, the adoring love for that first child is a deep, bottomless, endless, boundless, limitless well.

When my daughter, our oldest child, was four- months-old, I thought I was pregnant, and, although I knew I wanted more children eventually, I felt like I was betraying her at the time. It seemed too soon. My little girl was still a baby herself and needed all of me – how could I ever have enough love for two children? I wondered.

It turned out I was not expecting at that time; our second child was born when Rachel was 18-months-old. And I loved her just as deeply and strongly, and I also loved our second born, a son we named Ryan Christopher, just as deeply as my first born. There is enough love to go around.

Our family has grown to five children in 13 years. And I love them all individually, immensely, immeasurably, intensely. There is plenty of love. As God has enough love for each of His children, I too have such protective love for each of my children, but my love is never perfect like God's perfect love.

Even with my constant emphasis on how much I love and adore each of my children, there still are comments from the younger children at times of them wanting to be loved the most, and I never understand that. I always emphasize to my children how blessed they are to have one another, to have brothers and a sister. And I do think they know that, and will appreciate it even more as they get older.

At a spring gathering in our home for my daughter Rachel and her friends when they were in middle school, one of Rachel's pals remarks, "My brother is going off to college in September, and I will be all alone. I am so sad." Another friend agreed, "I know, my brother is leaving in a year. That's why I like coming here, there is so much going on."

That's for sure. Lots happening, lots of company, lots of laughter, lots of chaos, lots of craziness, lots of noise, lots of companionship. And lots of love. One thousand percent love for each child.

Kids and Politics – Refreshingly Innocent

My son's political t-shirt arrived in the mail last week, announcing who he wanted for president. Never mind that he's 11-years-old and won't be eligible to vote for seven years.

He's worn it every day since its arrival. At least my son makes sure it gets into the washer every day or two. At Bingo night at my children's school, a few moms came up to me who had seen my son wearing his t-shirt and said, "Good for Micki. That is so bold."

I am the chicken. As an adult I have been tamed by the realization that you have to be careful of partisan politics as they have become divisive. But, refreshingly, for kids it's just another day at school. Like asking which baseball team for which you are cheering.

My friend Kelly said she was listening to her 9-year-old son's conversation with another 9-year-old while carpooling to sports practice. The conversation went something like this: "So, who are you voting for?" "McCain," one says. "Don't you want change?" the other says. My friend is listening and just cracking up inside. The next minute the kids are talking about the upcoming game they will play on the weekend and homework that is due the next day and setting up a time to play after school.

I recently chaperoned a field trip for one of my twin fifth grade sons; while the boys were playing on their Nintendo DS's, they somehow were messaging each other on their DS's as to which candidate they wanted. It was "NoCain" then "NoBama" and my son was hiding from me what he was doing, and when I finally figured it out, I chuckled inside and said, "Make sure they are nice comments." The kids were fine about it all.

In high school, I was bold to stand up for a candidate who was not very popular in the polls – or in the school hallways – but ended up winning the presidency, and years later he is a respected president. I was not afraid to stand up for what I believed.

That is why I find my son's innocent campaigning for a candidate quite refreshing. Seeing children stick up for something they believe in is rewarding, as long as they are being respectful.

Maybe we could learn from our children's simplicity, and be able to state our opinions about political topics, then have a play date the following day.

Promise Me You Won't Forget

It is Sunday night about 10 p.m. I am tired. We just got back from being out of town. My baby Augustin, five-months-old, is fussing. I am trying to figure out if he is hungry or tired or thirsty or if he needs to be changed.

Our 5-year-old twin boys are still awake. I had asked our 11-year son to read to the boys before bed. It sure beats dishes when they are given a choice.

I try offering Baby Augustin some rice cereal, which we just started giving him this week, but he still fusses. I try nursing him then giving him a bottle to help settle him. I longed for rest, a moment to myself, to do a little quiet reading and writing, while all the kids were in bed. We had many late nights with kids up this summer.

As baby Augustin was calming down, the noise level in the older boys' rooms was rising, and I just knew they were not going to sleep. Sure enough, the twins zip upstairs for one more cup of water, and the question is popped.

"Mommy, can you read us a book and tuck us in?" twin Mickael Josef asks me.

Okay, guilt falls all over me as I think about wanting to have a moment to myself. I say, "Mickael Josef, I thought Ryan read to you and tucked you in. I'm feeding the baby."

"That's okay, you can come when you are finished," he says in that high pitched, sweet, innocent 5-year-old voice.

"Okay, sweetheart, of course I will; you go on downstairs, and I will be there as soon as possible," I say.

"Promise me Mom, you won't forget about it," Mickael Josef says.

Okay, now we are getting personal. How did he read my mind? Here is my 5-year-old, who was the baby of the family along with his twin brother just five months ago, and he is concerned about me forgetting about his request. Talk about a quick way to break a mom's heart. Never, ever, ever could I forget my sweet boy.

At bedtime over the years, we have a tuck in routine of reading the Bible or other books together and then praying. I would also sing them classic hymns like "Be Thou My Vision" or "Amazing Grace." I remember Ryan saying to me at bedtime when he was younger, "Mom, sing the 'I once was lost, now I am found' song." I also recited German poems about keeping the heart open for Jesus that they had learned by heart over the years, and we memorized John 3:16 together. Then when I leave the room, I remind my children to, "Read your Bible, and say your prayers."

My husband and I want to tuck our children in while

they still want to be tucked in. While they care about us not forgetting. I remember when Ryan was growing up, he'd ask, "Mom, can you tuck me in?" And I would say, yes of course. Then a few years later, the question changed to "Mom, I'm going to bed," and I took that as a hint that he wanted me to come downstairs to say good night to him, to tuck him in, but he did not ask directly. And my husband or I always would.

Then, and I do not remember when, but one day I realized my older son would go to bed without saying anything to me at all.

I recall Chris's dad saying, that for the first several years of a child's life, the child chases after the parents' affection, but then for the rest of the child's life, it is the parent chasing after the child.

I think about God, and how sometimes people think that He forgets about His children. Even when we get busy, He is chasing us. And, He promises, to never, ever, forget.

ADVENTURE

You are never too old to set another goal
or to dream a new dream.

- C.S. Lewis

Berry-Stained Hands

It was the smell of the ripe red strawberries and my berry-stained hands that transported me back to the summers of my childhood.

The month of June and the end of school meant it was fruit picking season for me. My family went U-picking at the various farms in the Portland area, gathering strawberries, raspberries, plums, cherries, and peaches.

Summers also meant berry picking for money. It was a summer ritual, much like going to the pool or hanging out with friends at the park or sleeping on the deck on our lounge chairs on hot summer nights.

I remember my berry-stained hands as a child, which wouldn't come clean no matter how hard I washed.

I was 11-years-old when I first started picking berries for money. The daily summer routine went something like this:

My sister and I would wake up with our alarm clocks, which jolted us out of bed at just past the crack of dawn; we would throw on old jeans over cutoff shorts before coming downstairs for breakfast, which lay before us on the table that my mom had set the night before for us. She made hard boiled eggs for us in the morning, and they were placed in these German porcelain egg holders. We had toast with our eggs and sometimes a bowl of cereal before grabbing our brown paper sack lunches from the refrigerator, adding a can of soda, with its bulging sides, from the freezer.

Then we meandered in the dawn mist to catch this rented school bus eight blocks away. The bus wound its way through our Portland city streets to the country, which seemed like it was so far away, but now I realize it was only Canby or Hillsboro. When we got to the dusty berry fields it was about 7 a.m. We went straight for the crates, which were stacked neatly in a row, and the field manager told us the rules: Pick your rows clean and don't throw berries.

When our rows weren't picked clean enough or when kids threw berries, the field manager would holler, "You know the rules!"

When you picked a crate full of berries, you got paid immediately. It was about $1.50 a crate for strawberries, depending on weight. We used to store our money in a plastic bag and count it at the end of the day.

I never did earn that much money at strawberry picking. I think that they probably actually lost money on me, because for every three strawberries I put in the crate, I would eat two.

Only problem was the John; yes, those wonderful out-houses in the berry fields. The outhouses were so bad that they kept my sister and her friends from eating any of the juicy red summer fruit while they picked.

Not me. I was born in June and I am a strawberry girl at heart, and I couldn't help myself. But it cost me. There I'd go, jumping the strawberry rows as if they were hurdles on an athletic track, making my way to those outhouses. They call them "honey buckets" today, but back then, they were anything but sweet. I remember them being filled with yellow jackets, not honey bees.

Berry picking for money was hard work. It was hot out in those fields, with no shade to shelter from the summer rays. It was dirty out there as well; the dust from the fields covered my clothes and face and hands.

But it was an experience that was a part of my Portland summers. Part of my childhood. It taught me to work hard earning money at a young age.

When my Corvallis friends Jeanie and Julie came to visit me in Portland, they would go berry picking with me, and to this day we talk about those years. My mom used to reward my friends by adding more days with us if we would go berry picking on additional days. How's that for entertaining your friends?

Although I valued berry picking as a summer youth job, it is something that my children and their friends will probably not be able to experience. Now there are laws keeping farmers from hiring children to pick berries. Newspaper articles report how local growers were fined for illegally employing children who were 12 and younger.

One article in a 1999 paper quoted an assistant district director for the United States Labor Department in Portland, Oregon as saying, "It surprised me, yes, to see them so young out there in the heat and the dust actually working and picking berries."

Well, flash backward, and there I was, "actually" working, picking berries. In the heat and the dust, actually.

Getting berry-stained hands.

And, ultimately, appreciating every minute of the adventure.

Except, maybe, those honey buckets.

Getting Beyond, Is It Safe?

A mom friend of mine and I were on an adventure hike at Tryon Creek State Park on Martin Luther King Junior Day with our children. She also has a 12-year-old son and we brought along our family's 12-year-old and 13-year-old friends from Sudan. My friend had not been to Tryon Creek – I so enjoy introducing other people to outdoor adventures with kids.

The four 12-year-old boys were meandering off the trail to discover trees that had fallen over the creek, and they wanted to walk over these trees to get to the other side.

At first I thought they should not go off the trail, but then I reasoned that there were no signs that indicated that going off the path was prohibited. Too many times at school and in life, kids are required to stay in bounds and live between the borders of walls and books and desks. But real life experiences happen best sometimes off the trail and outside of the lines and beyond the borders.

So, the boys took off down toward the tree which had fallen over the creek, and I followed them to make sure they were okay. Then, another woman who was also out for a hike at Tryon, stopped to see what the boys were doing, and asked my friend, "Is it safe?"

My mom friend said unashamedly to this woman, of course it is safe, and they are just boys on an adventure.

The woman's question, Is it safe? got me thinking about family life and safety and kids living in our suburban culture, where they are sheltered and not allowed to explore; and where parents drive their children everywhere instead of allowing them to walk or bicycle ride anywhere, because it is not safe. Ironically enough, because families move to the suburbs to be safe.

I think of Donald Miller's book, *A Million Miles in a Thousand Years*, where he ponders what makes a good story. Desire, goals, struggle, and risk come to mind. Miller points out that our lives are a story. I believe we need to get beyond thinking that God owes us a conflict-free existence. That will not happen this side of eternity.

It seems we forget that when life has risks and outside-the-box experiences and conflict, we grow as people, and we see our need for God. When we live our lives in the realm of adventure, when we take chances and try new things, we live lives where we are more dependent upon God.

Adults need adventure as much as kids do. My sister, who has nine children, and I have taken our kids over the years on hikes and various adventures during summer vacations and days off from school. On a particular hike to a waterfall at the Columbia River Gorge one year, our children discovered caves they could crawl into. They were thrilled. After they crawled back out, it was such a delight to listen to their excited conversation about the adventure of discovering a cave.

Children in Suburbia, USA need chances to crawl into caves and climb across trees that have fallen across creeks.

As my friend and I watched our 12-year-olds at Tryon Creek, we saw their eagerness to find log after log; and we saw team work as they tried to figure out the best way to make it across, and we saw their laughter and the challenge that it was. And we witnessed the excitement they expressed when they made it across the creek, each time waiting for one another to cross.

My 6-year-old wanted to join the older boys to cross the creek on these fallen trees, and I kept saying it is too hard and he kept getting upset at me for saying it was too hard. So on one tree that seemed reasonable for a 6-year-old to traverse, I said that we could cross it together; we tried, but then he got scared half way across the log so we turned around.

Then, on the next fallen tree he wanted to join the older boys again, so I took him, and we made it all the way across that time, and it was such a great adventure for him and me.

The challenge, the risk, the creativity, the team work, the maneuvering to find the best route were all skills that could be transferred to real life and real faith.

The boys got dirty and the trails were muddy and getting off the trails was even muddier, but the boys did not complain. They kept looking for more logs to cross.

The next day, I got a call from my mom friend, who said her son had an amazing time with us, and that is all he could talk about, the hike at Tryon Creek with my boys.

Was it safe? We weren't worried. And, most importantly, it was an adventure.

Can I Just Be There?

When our oldest son was 14-years-old, he spent almost two weeks in New Mexico at the Philmont Scout Ranch, backpacking in the Rockies with his dad, an assistant scoutmaster, and other West Linn Boy Scout Troop 149 scouts and leaders.

Philmont Scout Ranch is Boy Scouts of America's premier high-adventure destination that challenges hikers on over 200 square miles of rugged New Mexico wilderness.

During my husband and son's Philmont Boy Scout experience, they explored the great outdoors in one big adventure, something vital to true living: getting away from electronics, amplified noise and schedules; setting daily physical goals of reaching a certain destination and then accomplishing it; and just appreciating what they might come across as they backpacked two to 10 miles a day.

While my husband and oldest son traipsed through the wilderness of New Mexico, I decided to do a little adventuring as well. I was thinking of a road trip. So, my daughter, the twins, and I took off together while 3-year-old Augustin stayed with grandma and grandpa. For our getaway, we had a few destinations in mind – to visit family in Idaho and my college friend Meri in the Bay area – and we also just wanted to see what we could discover along the way. There is nothing like that feeling of getting away together for a long journey. We navigated with our maps, enjoyed the sweet long hours in the car, and savored the scenery and those we visited.

We need adventure, exploring, away from our suburban parameters and "have-to's" that life places on us.

It doesn't need to be two weeks away. My husband took our twin sons when they were 8-years-old on a two-day backpacking trip in the Jefferson wilderness area. And our family goes camping at Timothy Lake near Mount Hood each year, where we take the john boat out on the lake to catch crawdads and fish, and where we hike in the wilderness and where we roast marshmallows under the stars. All adventure.

Adventure is about being there and discovering along the way, exploring. On a family bicycle ride one year at Salmon Creek near Vancouver, Washington, Ryan eyed a snake and just had to stop and pick it up. He has a radar that spots slithering creepy creatures that move along the ground or hide in bushes.

The twins are the same way. Their brakes screeched to a halt when they saw Ryan holding the snake, and they insisted on a turn holding it. Later that day, the boys spotted a frog in a creek along the trail where we had meandered.

I enjoy the change of pace in the summer, getting away from the feel of the school year where kids have to sit in chairs in neat little rows and raise their hands to speak; and where children are told to be careful when running on the playground and to walk in a straight line, and where parents plan neat little play dates for after school.

Sometimes, parents have a tendency to book kids for camps during the summer to keep the chaos and craziness and squabbling to a minimum. But kids also need unstructured time where not every last minute is packed with sports practices and music lessons and clubs. One mom I talked with recently remembers twirling her baton for hours outside as a child while daydreaming. Let's bring back daydreaming, unstructured time.

During summer months, I began making a deliberate goal to go on a new outdoor adventure each week. It takes slowing down and retuning and retraining ourselves and our kids. I later blog about it on my website.

When my husband took our daughter in 2008 on a week adventure to search for wild horses in Eastern Oregon, I took our older three boys on an adventure of our own. We had few plans, which did not sit well at first for Ryan, who was almost an Eagle Scout by then, but he went along for the journey. We hiked Sleeping Beauty Trail in Trout Lake, Washington, near a missions camp I wanted to check out, and then we camped at a campground next to a creek. The next day we drove to Long Beach, Washington to spend the night.

Adventure means surprises and drawing outside of the lines and filling in the blanks ourselves. Being totally there, in the moment.

When a mom friend of mine asked her teenage daughter to call every day while she would be away at a camp one summer, the daughter said something profound: "Can I just be there?"

Adventure is about just that – being there.

Africa Came to Me - Living the Dream

I was recently talking with another soccer mom about my daughter Rachel being in Germany pursuing her dreams. Rachel is in language school so she can pass the German proficiency language exam required for admission into the German university system.

Right out of high school she also went to Europe, first to Germany then Austria, attending Bible College – affiliated with the Torchbearers Bible Schools, a dream of hers that she fulfilled. Rachel had the chance to travel to various European countries and continues the adventure there while in school.

This mom friend that I was talking to about Rachel being in Europe said to me, "I think it is wonderful that your daughter is following her dreams to go to Europe after high school." This mom said that she too had a dream to travel overseas after she graduated, and to join the Peace Corps, but instead she heeded the advice of her parents and well meaning adults to first go to college and get her career going. Then travel.

It's been 20 plus years and this mom still feels she has unfulfilled dreams to live.

My husband had a dream to travel across the country in his Fiat Spider convertible after he graduated from the University of Portland with his mechanical engineering degree. He wanted to take five weeks to camp along the way, bring his guitar and sing at campfires, and meet people to share Christ with them. That was his vision.

While interviewing for jobs after graduation, he noted to his potential employers that, though he was serious about his career and starting as soon as possible, he would be taking this cross-country trip with his convertible when mid-summer hit, and he would need five weeks off of work, unpaid, to travel.

Some potential employers said to him, "Call us when you are serious about working." One company, though, saw my husband's potential and hired him (Blount, International). And sure enough, after Chris had been working for a few months, once summer hit he took off to fulfill his dream of traveling across the country in his Fiat convertible.

He returned to work, dream fulfilled, and has continued to work for Blount for 25 years; he's earned 10 patents for the company so far. God honored him for following his dream.

I so enjoyed the recent Disney movie UP! In it a young creative Carl dreams of adventure and he meets a spirited Ellie, also a dreamer, both promising one another that they would travel to a lost land in South America. It is their dream. The film moves quickly through their lives – marriage, saving for their dream trip, bills to pay, bad news on not being able to have children, saving for the trip, more bills to pay, graying hair. And, still, no dream fulfilled.

Then, Ellie dies, and Carl remembers his promise to her. With the inspiration from a Boy-Scout-like- 8-year-old boy named Russell, Carl lives his dream to reach South America. The message? It is never too late to go after your dreams.

I also had a dream: To travel to Africa between semesters of college, to learn about maybe becoming a Wycliffe Bible translator. When I told my parents I wanted to go to Africa, they did not discourage me, but they did advise that I first get my college degree.

I got my degree. Then, I got married. Had kids. I have not been to Africa – yet.

Yes, I am doing other good things and I feel God has given me new dreams; and I am so blessed to raise my five amazing children and I feel like God is allowing me to make a difference in the community where I have been placed. And I continually pray for God to direct me and my family's lives.

But, I have not been to Africa. I am not saying I am not living the life God would have me live, and I know I prayed a lot for God's direction in my life when I was younger. All I am saying is my advice to my children and to others: Live the dream now. Don't get stuck in a prescribed life. Ask questions. Dream big dreams. Follow those dreams. Live the

130

adventure. While you are young. While the dreams are still vivid and strong.

I know you can also live the dream when you are older with kids and a spouse and a job, but it just gets harder. I do believe in restored dreams and new dreams and never forgetting those original dreams.

And sometimes childhood dreams change and that is part of life as well. Maybe God allows us to live our dreams in a different format and shape.

Take my Africa dream. Through a church ministry we met a Sudan refugee family of nine in 2006 who lived in North Portland and who had no beds or couches and or dining room table. We were able to help them out and networked with others in our church and community to assist as well. We have continued to stay in touch with them, and they are a big part of our lives; we've celebrated Christmas and Easter together; we've taken them to the beach and to the mountains; we've hosted sports camps in their neighborhoods and shared meals; we've brought them to church and the children to youth group, and kids have stayed with us over weekends. My kids like playing with their kids. They are our friends.

Yes, I still have a dream to go to Africa. And, my adventuresome daughter also has a heart for Africa and wants to travel there. Maybe someday I can join her.

For now, Africa came to me.

CELEBRATION

If your daily life seems poor, do not blame it; blame yourself that you are not poet enough to call forth its riches; for the Creator, there is no poverty.

- Rainer Maria Rilke

Mother's Day

When I was a little girl, Daddy pulled us aside a week before Mother's Day, and spoke in a whisper: "Next week is Mother's Day; can you make Mama a card? Here are paper and markers."

So every year, we found a spot in my professor-dad's home office, complete with floor to ceiling book shelves, and we'd craft a hand-written card in German with the words, *Herzlichen Gluckwunsch zum Mutter Tag* (*Happy Mother's Day*). *And* Daddy asked us to think of reasons we were thankful for Mama.

"Thank you for speaking German to me and for sacrificing so much for your children," I often wrote. Or, "Thank you for teaching me the value of hard work."

Then my brother, sister, Daddy and I would walk to the local Fred Meyer on Hawthorne Street to purchase a gift for

Mama, often a flower she could plant or an item she'd hinted at needing for the kitchen. It was our way of showing gratitude to her on Mother's Day. As we got older, we used our own money for gifts.

On the day of the celebration, Daddy would take us all out to dinner or we would celebrate with home-made waffles, and surround Mama with her gifts and cards.

Honoring our mother each year on Mother's Day was something that happened mostly because of our father. Celebrating our mom on Mother's Day had become such a participatory tradition for us children, that when we all eventually moved out on our own, we continued doing something to honor Mama on Mother's Day. A gift, maybe a brunch out or dinner together. A hand-written card with a personalized sentiment.

And, now being a Mom myself, my husband does for me what my dad did for my mom.

I know some men say, "She's not *my* mom." Others say: "It's just another Hallmark Holiday." While these things may be true, I say Mother's Day is still a perfect opportunity to do something nice for the one who brings life into the world.

Each year, my husband takes our children aside, either shopping at the store or more recently, creating a craft and card of some kind together.

For Mother's Day 2005, my husband spent a good part of a Saturday, right after we returned from baseball with the twins, working on a project with the kids.

"The garage is off limits to you today," he said to me teasingly.

The children dashed secretively in and out of the garage between trips to the backyard to bounce on the trampoline with their cousin.

"No peeking Mommy," 7-year-old twins Mickael Josef and Wesley reminded me with playful voices as they whiplashed past me in the kitchen.

Then, on Mother's Day, after church, my five children gathered around our dining room table, surrounding me with brightly colored packages and huge smiles. I took turns with each child, opening up their hand-made gifts.

From 2-year-old Augustin: A bumble bee wooden fridge magnet, painted bright yellow and black, and a photograph of him posing in a field of forget-me-nots is glued on top.

"Augustin is your buzzing bee," my husband told me as I admired the crafty magnet. My little 2-year-old was so proud of his creation as I admired his handiwork and thanked him.

Next, I unwrapped a wooden tulip magnet from Mickael Josef; a star and purple dress magnet from Wesley (the purple dress one was made at school); tree and seashell magnets from 13-year-old Ryan; and a handmade bead necklace from my artist daughter Rachel, 15.

My husband also orchestrated another craft: making photograph ornaments, where on one side the kids had painted, "I love you," and "Happy Mother's Day," while on the other side was a photograph of each child, taken in the field of forget-me-nots in our backyard.

And, the hand-made cards that accompanied the gifts were pure poetry to me.

"To Mom, From Wesley, I love you! I love you! You are the best Mommy! You are nice. I love you very much."

And from Micki: "Mom, you are very, very, very, very, very, very, very, very, very, nice. You are the best Mom. You are a good Mom!"

My teenagers are more practical: "Dear Mom, Happy Mother's Day. I love your cookies and coffee cake. Thank you for bringing me to band every morning. Love Ryan."

"Dear Mom, I love you. Rachel."

And, also from Mickael Josef, a Handprint Mom poem written at school for me, one that I recognized from my older children's school years, that tugs at my heart afresh:

"Dear Mom, these are the prints you've seen before. On the bathroom wall and refrigerator door. Those you remove so graciously, These you keep for memory. Love, Micki."

After I had opened up my handmade presents and cards, created with the encouragement of my husband (and my kids' teachers), it was time for a Mother's Day meal.

"Anywhere you want to go," my husband told me.

So we drove along the Columbia River Gorge, to Mosier, Oregon, population 430, for a Mother's Day late lunch at the Wildflower Café with my sweet family, an eatery that I read about in the newspaper's Travel section. I savored the Hungarian mushroom soup and salad with dill-yogurt dressing while listening to the sweet music of five children chattering.

Next, I wanted to go on a hike and look for wildflowers. We meandered along the Old Columbia River Gorge Highway, now a bicycle and walking path, and the children darted ahead, able to run freely. It was as if God orchestrated the timing of Mother's Day to coordinate with the majestic blooming of wildflowers to smile on Moms – Bachelor's Button, Balsamroot, Lupine, and California Poppy graced the path and meadows.

At the end of the day, I thanked my children individually for my special Mother's Day.

And my husband as well.

The Value of Traditions

Every ornament is a celebration.

It is a symphony of children saying, almost singing, "Oh look at this, I was a baby here." "Mommy, is this one mine?" "Wow, look at all the pretty colors." "Our tree's going to be so awesome." "Our tree is so beautiful." "Oh, here's another one." "Look, an angel."

We're decorating our nine-foot noble Christmas tree, the one we found in the snowy mountains the weekend of Thanksgiving. Our tradition.

We're listening to our Christmas CD's while adorning our Tannenbaum, smelling fresh pine, seeing lights go up, touching the prickly branches.

Each ornament we place on the tree blankets us with memories. An East Coast historical trip in 1988, pre-kids. Europe, 1989, again pre-kids. Baby's first Christmas, 1990, for Rachel, who is now in sixth grade. Ryan's ornament from

140

second grade with his 7-year-old smiling face plastered on Popsicle sticks glued together with glitter glue. The twin's picture in a "First Christmas" ornament given to them by their Grandma in 1997. They were two-months-old in the photograph. They are now 4-years-old.

Other ornaments remind us of family vacations we've taken together. Road trips to Yosemite and Lake Tahoe. Spring break at Cannon Beach. Some bring memories of school days and others of Sunday School; and some were created at ornament making parties with friends and neighbors and cousins and siblings.

Traditions. Christmas holiday customs. How important they are to families. Searching for the perfect noble Christmas tree every year in the woods. Making homemade roll out cookies using my Mom's recipe. Baking cinnamon rolls. Buying a gift for Angel Tree prison inmates' children. Singing Christmas carols at church. Creating homemade ornaments and gifts. Decorating the tree.

Letting the children set up the hand carved wooden manger scene, while listening to them talk of the baby Jesus being born in Bethlehem. Taking in Christmas specials on DVD's, dancing and singing to Mister Grinch and Rockin' Around the Christmas Tree. Strolling down Peacock Lane in Portland in awe of the beautifully lit houses.

Experiencing the Nutcracker, Handel's Messiah, living nativity scenes and Christmas concerts. Reaching out to others to help make their Christmas memorable. Having the children open up a chocolate a day in their German Advents calendar. Lighting an Advent candle the four weeks before Christmas and reading a segment of the Christmas story in the Bible. Attending Christmas Eve church service as a family. Reading the nativity story in the Book of Luke on Christmas Eve.

I remember Christmas Eve growing up in my German family, eating Red Snapper that had been dipped in egg and bread crumbs and Cornflakes then fried, accompanied with my mom's homemade potato salad. Then we all went upstairs while the "ChristKind" (Christ child) delivered presents underneath the tree. My parents would ring the bell and we'd come downstairs to a Christmas tree lit with candles and we'd sing "Ihr Kinderlein Kommet," (O Come Little Children) and "Stille Nacht," (Silent Night); then my parents would read the story of the birth of Christ in the book of Luke out loud to us before we opened presents. That tradition is one my husband and I now carry on with our family in similar fashion with cousins and grandparents and even neighbors over.

And we have carried on my husband's family's tradition of driving to the Mount Hood National Forest the day after Thanksgiving to search for our Christmas Tree in the woods.

When I led a writing workshop for students at Rosemont Ridge Middle School, I asked participants to write about holiday memories; one sixth grader said he had no family Christmas traditions. But when I probed deeper, he began explaining the moment he and his siblings stir on Christmas morning, they wake their parents and open their presents, which are neatly arranged under the tree. I told him that is a tradition. Write about it.

We need to talk to our children about the stories. To

use the word, tradition. And beyond the holidays, it is important to create other family traditions. We have a Friday pizza and movie night the kids look forward to each week. Traditions and routines give kids a reason to be home. And a reason to bring their friends over. I remember going to my husband's parent's house each Sunday night for their family dinners when we were dating and which we continued doing after we were married until their schedules changed.

I met a woman and her mom at the pool and I talked about traditions with them. The mom recalls their family's tradition of frying hamburgers and making homemade French fries every Saturday evening. It was so simple, yet so meaningful.

Like celebrating every ornament on the Christmas tree.

Packed Parking Lots and
Christmas Cheer

I was trying to find a parking space in the Costco lot
the Sunday after Thanksgiving, as I needed a birthday pres-
ent for my nephew. I'm vying for that perfect location near
the front doors, which is not to be found in the sea of cars
and SUV's, so I settle for a far off location, figuring the
walk will do me good. As I dodge speeding vans walking to
the entryway, I wonder if cash may have been the wiser
choice of a gift.

But instead, I was stuck with the crowds doing their
Christmas shopping on the busiest commerce-spending
weekend of the season.

When inside, I decide that I might as well look around
to see what I might need for the holiday season. I'm always
looking for the perfect gift for family members. When I get
to the clothes area, I see these great deals on men's brand
name shirts, perfect for my father. But then I remember:
The last shirts I gave him still sit unwrapped in the family

room. He assures me he will wear them someday when his other ones are worn out.

My parents are just not ones to be wasteful. They grew up during the war in Europe and have known hard times. Once you've known what it's like to be without, it is hard to be extravagant. When I grew up – forget Kleenex – we used toilette paper for our noses. And our used napkins from dinner out at Round Table Pizza ended up in our bathroom for secondary purposes.

And, I can still see my dad as a college professor at the University of Portland with his wide-as-a-river ties when the style was razor thin. His students teased him playfully, and he'd have some fun in return, saying that they needed to just wait and see: in 10 years, he'd be setting the trends. And sure enough, wide ties came back, and there my dad was right up there style-wise with designer Ralph Lauren.

One year for Christmas, I gave my parents a new coffee maker with all the bells and whistles. Their old model wouldn't heat up water any more, and you practically had to jump start the thing to get hot brown water, and you felt that at any moment the loose handle would give way and you'd be cleaning up a billion pieces of glass from the broken carafe.

Well, a month after giving my folks the state-of-the-art coffee maker, we came over for dinner; and when my mom went to make the after-dinner cup of Joe, she used — you guessed it — Old Faithful. The new machine was sitting in the family room, in its unopened original box, right next to a pile of brand new men's shirts that I — and my brother and sister – had given my dad over the years.

In our generation, especially around the holidays, we can have a tendency to overindulge our children as we try to find the latest trinket for underneath the tree. Things they probably do not need.

Lately, we've been skipping the many Costco trips around the holidays, and instead crafting homemade presents to give to one another and to others during the Christmas season. It saves money, which we can use to help those in need.

The idea for simplifying Christmas and using money saved to help others came from the Advent Conspiracy, begun by Imago Dei Community. It saves lives — and nerves — something we all could use this time of year. Especially when dodging speeding cars in packed parking lots.

MILESTONES AND TRANSITIONS

Prayer

At some point you pray
Not because you've made it

Not because you see the stony hand opening before
but because somewhere the sky leans a familiar grey
into the trees and they acknowledge it
reweaving the shroud of their deep roots

Nothing particular happens in you –
the sky becomes a still white mound
and you find your knees suddenly wanting down.

                                                    - Emma Howell

The Golden Years are Now

When our two oldest children were in middle school one year, they were missing from our New Year's Eve celebration for the first time. They had been invited to separate gatherings at the homes of friends and the whole evening felt different. All evening I kept thinking about them, wondering what they were doing at different moments.

And when the clock struck midnight and my husband was out blowing our seventh grader's Boy Scout bugle without him there, and letting off fireworks with our 6-year-old twins, I kept feeling something was missing. It is just not the same when we are not all together.

For the past 13 years, we have always spent New Year's eves with all of our children together.

When our 13-year-old first asked me to go elsewhere on New Year's Eve, I said, "We have family plans, to go to grandma's and our family friends are also coming this year."

"I know," my daughter replied with a tad bit of hesitation, "but I really want to go to my friend's this year."

"But it's a tradition to celebrate together," I offer.

She persists, "Can I go?"

"Okay."

A day later my son got a call as well from his friend Jon. "Yes, you can also go."

Each January as we turn the calendar to a new year, we see the changes in our children, the monuments that illustrate how they are growing and moving from one stage to another.

The changes are never over night – they take place over time – but when we notice them we then say, "It was only yesterday when..." or "Remember how you used to..."

I have to practice the art of letting go gracefully.

I've been noticing a difference in my 6-year-old twins lately as well. I was leaving the house for a "girls' party" at a neighbor's house this holiday season and I announced to the boys, "I'm leaving now," as I looked back at them.

Silence. I try again. "Goodbye Wesley and Mickael Josef. I'll be back in a couple of hours."

No pitter-patter of feet racing for the door.

No "Mommy, wait, I want to give you a hug good bye."

Nothing.

Just a simple, casual, grown-up, "Bye Mom" as they continued playing their game.

150

I used to try to be inconspicuous when I had to go somewhere, to sneak out without a big to-do about my leaving, because I was usually in a hurry and they'd hold me up with, "Mommy I need a hug," or "Wait Mom, I need to kiss you on the cheek," and "now the other cheek." And they'd ask "Where are you going Mom?" and "When are you coming home?" and "Can I go with you?" and they'd say, "Wave to me, and keep waving to me."

Now that they are 6-years-old they have slowly stopped doing that. Their world is larger.

Each year, I have new examples of these transformations, these milestones.

My mother- in-law says to me, "These are the golden years you are living, right now. They are not when you are retired – they are now, while raising your children."

These are the golden years, hearing a high-pitched tone, "Mommy" as my children run to greet me when I come home, as if they haven't seen me in weeks when I have only been gone for a couple of hours. These are the golden years, reading to my children at night, hearing bedtime prayers and getting sweet hugs with tiny fingers wrapped around me.

The golden years are the everyday of life, when we are our children's worlds.

Our children's worlds will change and grow larger, and it is always my prayer that they know they will always be my world.

Teenage Driver

When my daughter, Rachel, a freshly minted 16-year-old, got her driver's license in late February, her "I'm free" wings sprouted immediately. "Can I borrow the car to drive to Red Robin tonight for a going-away party for an exchange student?" she asked.

"You mean at night?" I asked anxiously, "by yourself in a car?"

"Well, I would be caravanning with Chelsea," she added, "that way you and Dad can relax tonight and not have to pick me up."

"Relax" is not the first thing that comes to mind when I think of my first child on the road at night in a car by herself. And it's not necessarily Rachel's driving skills I'm concerned about so much as all the reckless drivers out there.

We decided to not let her drive to Red Robin, opting instead to drive her there ourselves. We are easing into this whole independent-borrow-the-car-especially-at-night stage cautiously.

"Right now, driving to the local video store and picking up your brothers at their friends' houses will be the extent of your wings' reach," my husband told Rachel at the beginning.

One evening, we let Rachel go a short distance to and from her dance team practice at West Linn High School; after the scheduled practice had been over for 25 minutes and my daughter still was not home, I became restless.

Then we heard a siren and the phone rang and my worst nightmare fear went into high gear. I prayed so hard.

The call was from a friend just saying hello, and seconds later, we welcomed the sound of our garage door opening. "Did you stop by a friend's on your way home?" I asked my daughter.

"No. I stopped at the store," Rachel said. Okay, New Rule, I announced. "Call us — but not while driving — if you are going to stop somewhere and come home later than expected. That's why we got you a cell phone."

On a recent Saturday morning, we let Rachel borrow the car to drive to track practice at Tryon Creek State Park in Lake Oswego.

"I love the freedom," she said, jingling the keys as she scurried to the car, telling me she drives with the music loud. "Okay, another rule. Don't drive with the music blaring," I warned. "It distracts you."

About the time she should have been home from track practice, my cell phone rang. "Can I go with Chelsea and a bunch of others to Noah's Bagels?" "Yes. Thanks for letting

153

me know, Sunshine." The first rule was working, having her call me if she is delayed.

Back at home, Rachel said, "Aren't you glad I can drive now, and I can be more independent? It's easier for you. You don't have to worry about taking me anymore."

No more worries? The real worrying is just beginning. I know it is all a part of the letting go process, as so much of parenting is. Transitions. To place her in God's hands and care. To pray a lot and to have faith.

I think of how God wants us to let go and to trust Him. The passage in the Bible where Jesus asks Peter to let go and walk toward Him on the water is about faith. And trust. Peter did let go. But I am guessing not without a lot of prayer.

The Long Good-Bye

I wanted to savor every moment, every train trip, every sip of cappuccino, every conversation, every new city we explored, every smile with my daughter. We had two weeks and one day before I had to say good bye to her. Sometimes just thinking about leaving her made me cry. Sometimes I just sobbed. But, I would not let her see me. It would be too hard.

On her. And on me.

She chose to go to Bodenseehof, a Bible College in Germany, during her first year beyond high school, and I was delighted. Germany is the country of my birth. My mother-in-law had asked me at one point: "Why are you encouraging Rachel to go so far away to school."

What I encouraged my daughter to do and what I emphasize with my four other children is to seek after God's will in their lives. To find their purpose. Their calling. To risk. To venture out. To question. To live outside-the-box once in a while. To journey. To dream.

And for Rachel, going to Germany this first year out of high school was her dream.

The reality of it though hit me about half way through our two weeks of traveling before I was to drop her off at Bible College.

We had had our first few days of seeing Buckingham Palace, London Bridge, Dusseldorf, family gatherings, cathedrals in Cologne.

It had been of course amazing so far, yet at times it felt a bit hectic always being on the go. And my daughter said something to me that stuck: "We haven't sat down and had torte—German for cake—and coffee at a café."

And I realized that what matters to Rachel is not having to see every cathedral or church or museum there is in every town.

No, what's important to my daughter is sipping cappuccinos at sidewalk cafes, walking on cobblestone streets, bicycle riding around town, running through fields of wildflowers, and searching for open spaces. That is what stays with her.

And here, our first few days, though really great, we sometimes didn't stop for meals until really late at night. Or we'd skip lunch. And this got to my daughter. I wanted the memories that Rachel would take from our trip – from these two weeks together before I dropped her off at Bodenseehof — to be wonderful. Sweet. Happy.

So, I changed directions in my mind. I decided that it was not so much about the finding but it was about the journey. The very thing I talk about in life often. The adventure.

As we continued on our two weeks, we made sure that at the first hint of being tired or hungry we found a place to sit and eat. Or have Italian ice. Or sip cappuccinos in cafes on cobblestone streets. Or watch the sunset along the river.

We did not see everything there is to see in Europe. Just to be there was of course fascinating, but I allowed myself to not be on such an agenda-setting course, where you forget to smell the roses.

I wanted to savor every moment before the inevitable goodbye.

When we arrived at Bodenseehof in Friedrichshafen where I was to leave Rachel, we walked along Lake Constance with Helga and Norbert, my cousins who had driven us there, and I was able to see Rachel's room and meet the staff and a few students at the school. I snapped her photograph in front of the sign that said, Bodenseehof. And we hugged and I prayed for her.

Then I asked if I should go back into the hall with her and she politely said, "That's okay Mom," which was my sign to go out gracefully. I turned to give her another hug and I could feel the tears welling up in me, but I did not want to cry in front of her. Not that I cannot show emotion in front of my daughter, but it was time for me to let go. To say good-bye.

I had prepared her 18 and half years for this, and she was ready. Was I?

LIFE LESSONS

Every person above the ordinary has a certain mission that they are called to fulfill.

- Johann Wolfgang von Goethe

Kids Need to Feel That They are Loved

The phone rings and I can tell it will be a work call I need to concentrate on, so I tip-toe into my bedroom and close the door, but somehow I am discovered – my littlest one, then 4-years-old, follows me into my room like a magnet, and then my twins, 10-years-old, crash in as well, hopping onto my bed, laughing and jumping.

I let them bounce on my bed, even though they should not, as I slip back out of my room, but all of a sudden jumping on my bed is not fun anymore; my children follow me out of my bedroom, all the while ignoring my glares that tell them: Mom is in the middle of an important call and they should be quieter.

Later, I talk to my husband about being followed everywhere I go and he teases me playfully, "You're so loved," as I roll my eyes and smile, and he adds, "You always wanted shadows."

Our youngest will start kindergarten this fall. Registration forms are due now, and I am trying to figure out whether to put him in all-day or half-day. My husband wants us to register him for half-day. "He's so young. Keep him home with you longer," he says. He notes how sweet and innocent our youngest is, and that he is not ready to hit the big world for a full day of school every day.

Age four truly is precious, and I tell my little boy while tucking him in that I love him so much; and he knows he is getting older — he'll be five next month – and he also knows that my heart is torn because he won't be my little baby anymore. He looks at me with his deep chocolate brown eyes and says with giggles, "I'm getting bigger and bigger."

I tease him: "No, I won't let you get bigger. I am going to hold you down."

He says, "Well, my feet are getting bigger." I take his feet and squish them.

He says, "Well, my tummy is getting bigger," and I take his tummy and squeeze it.

He says, "Well, my hands are getting bigger," and I take his hands and squeeze them, saying I won't let them get bigger.

It is our little song and dance. I tell him to not turn five so quickly, and he says to me, "I have to – I get my knife." A guy tradition with his dad.

I think he knows in his little pre-school way how important he is to me, and I also think he *feels* how important he is to me.

Kids need that. To not only know they are our world, but to *feel* it. That is the thing. As parents, we want to communicate both verbally and non-verbally to our children that they are the most important, most valued, most beautiful human beings in our lives. That no matter what happens – friends leaving, people changing, jobs transitioning – Mom and Dad are there – and they love you.

Even when they are trying to get away for a moment of peace on the telephone.

Life is about More than Winning

While attending my son and daughter's High School District Cross Country meet in October, a boy was minutes behind the others in the eleventh and twelfth grade JV race. I noticed him as he ambled along the last 100 yards on the track, in front of the stadium that would later hold crowds cheering for the top finishers. He, though, would take home no trophies.

What kept him going, I wondered, as he hobbled to the finish line in dead last place? Most spectators didn't even realize a competitor remained on the course until this boy appeared. We were all waiting for the awards ceremony.

It made me think about kids – and adults – who go through life unnoticed, the quiet average people, who continue day in and day out living their lives without fanfare. Something more than recognition and winning keeps them going.

I've always felt for the underdog, for the one who doesn't get the trophy or the solo part or the lead in the play, but instead remains in the background, as a support to the stars. Then, there are the volunteers who show up weekly in schools and the neighbor who visits the shut-ins daily. The shy guy who, if you take the time to get to know, you'd see is a gem. The Sunday School teacher that has mentored hundreds of kids through the Bible. And the Boy Scout leader who has helped dozens of Scouts navigate their way through the wilderness of life toward the Eagle award.

When my son Ryan was an eighth grader, his jazz band met every morning except Fridays to practice before school, and they played at school assemblies and functions throughout the year; yet, when he brought home his yearbook in June and I thumbed through looking for the jazz band photograph, there was none. No recognition for these dedicated musicians, while the sports teams received full page spreads.

During the fall, cross country has always played second fiddle to football, soccer and volleyball when it comes to media coverage. When my daughter was in tenth grade, she said to me, "Mom, cross country had no article or photo again in the newspaper this week, and we are rated fifth in State. The other sports are never left out."

I felt for her, and added, "Just enjoy when the team *is* in the paper. When I went to Cleveland High in Portland and ran cross country, we rarely got a story or photo in the paper."

Of course, my daughter and son weren't running to be featured in the newspaper; they were participating for the joy of the sport, the excitement of competition, the satisfaction of being on a team and improving individually. All season, they cheered for each member of the team, whether they were first or 51st.

Head West Linn High Cross Country Coach Scott Spear said: "It can't be all about winning, because in life you can do your very best and not even get recognized for your efforts let alone win. Our focus is for us to take risks, push ourselves, and compete the best we can."

Is that not precisely how life is? Doing what you need to do, vigilantly, when no camera flashes in your face. Our true character shines through when no one is observing. As it says in the Word, "Do your work heartily as to the Lord rather than man."

Marathon-Length Goals

I came from a family of runners. We attended weekend road races all year, and all-comers track meets in the summer; my siblings and I ran cross country and track during the school year. And, my dad and my sister both ran marathons, but for some reason that did not interest me.

Until now.

A friend of mine, who has run his fair share of marathons, asked me why I never have competed in the 26.2 mile feat. Maybe it was my past knee injuries from running and playing basketball in my younger years. And perhaps kids had more recently kept me from it. His reaction impacted me: Be careful not to use kids as an excuse in my life.

That got to me. I realize, moms need to keep having goals of our own.

So one day, I began walking at 5:30 in the morning, every day, working my way up to running, and then the thought of completing a marathon entered my mind. My friend Kristi, also a mom, had run/walked several marathons. After months of getting up at 5:30 a.m. on pitch-dark cold mornings, I decided I could do this, too. I could have a goal and train towards this accomplishment of physical endurance. Yes, even I, a mom of four children at the time. I decided to register for the Portland Marathon, and continued training until the day when I joined over 7,000 runners and walkers and wheelchair users on a glorious Sunday morning in downtown Portland, Oregon. Thousands of people were clapping and cheering on the 26-mile course and hundreds of volunteers handed out Gatorade and bananas and other energy food. No matter where you were on the course and no matter how fast or slow you were going, you truly felt like you were a winner.

Because the marathon is not just a physical test, but it is a mental challenge. In the end, you are your only competitor. You feel good just to have accomplished such an athletic adventure of the body.

My daughter, who was one of the volunteers with her Girl Scout troop, gave me my rose as I crossed the finish line. We also received a medal and a t-shirt, which I now wear as a trophy.

The rest of my family was waiting for me at the end as well. It was wonderful to have them all there to cheer me on. It is good for kids to see their mom (and dad) have goals that they complete. I have cheered on so many of my kids' events, and there is value in them being there to cheer on their mom.

168

I was so happy to finish it. It was one of the hardest things I have done in my life. Afterwards, I wore my marathon t-shirt everywhere. A pastor at my church saw my shirt and said he ran 18 miles of the marathon one year, but then dropped out without finishing it. He said he had gotten off pace and decided it was too hard to finish.

I thought, wow, to run that far and to not finish. Unless I was injured, I would force myself to complete the course, even if I knew I would not be able to reach my specific goal of completing the event in a certain amount of time.

The marathon is like life. It is hard work, you have to sweat a little, and you need nourishment along the way. And like life, it is not necessarily that you complete it perfectly, but just that you complete it whole heartily. It is nice to be cheered on, but in the end no one can do it for you. It is something you do for yourself, to reach a goal, to say, I did it.

After my first marathon, I have run/walk five additional ones. I have encouraged other mom friends of mine to compete in marathons with me. I have asked my children to join me. In 2008, my daughter ran the Newport Marathon with me. She ran cross country during her high school years, and still said the marathon was one of the hardest things she has accomplished athletically. I was glad to be able to do this together.

Like life, it was very much worth the effort.

Mississippi Miracle

While on the flight to New Orleans with my two oldest kids, Rachel and Ryan, for a seven–day church mission trip/ youth group summer camp to the Katrina-devastated region, the woman, Ashley, next to me, a film maker based in Mississippi, was intrigued by our 200-member team. "I have made two documentaries on Hurricane Katrina," the film maker noted. "And our church has hosted many relief groups in Katrina-rebuild efforts."

"But people have stopped coming. They have forgotten about us, so you are an answer to prayer. Thank you for coming," Ashley said graciously.

We found that gratitude repeated many times during our entire experience in Moss Point, Mississippi, where my two high school children and I joined our church youth group to partner with Pastor Jerry of New Covenant

Community Ministries and Forward Edge International in Hurricane Relief efforts, and that gratefulness rubbed off on us.

For starters, came the greeting at the airport at midnight by dozens of church members, along for the two-hour journey back to Moss Point. Then, on our first morning, we were primed to begin painting in a local school, but instead were welcomed with an assembly of people in the auditorium. Colorful balloons, welcome signs, a band playing music, city dignitaries, the local press, church leaders and school officials – all gathered to thank us for coming. It was like one of those high school pep rallies where the victorious football team walks into a cheering crowd.

Community and church leaders warmly greeted us, telling us how they admired us for giving of our time. After the festivities, our painting duties began, and teachers and school officials came by throughout the week to again offer thanks.

We, however, would realize that we were the ones who needed to do the thanking.

In the evenings, the church folks gathered to serve us meals, supper that they started preparing early in the day. Hand-dipped catfish for 200 plus people; home-made macaroni and cheese; fried chicken; and sweet tea to wash it down. They were always smiling and never complained about cooking all day – they just selflessly served us, modeling true hospitality.

Several groups of youth each day had the chance to assist in church-sponsored sports camps, where we drove to the projects to pick up children. Those children, who were living in poverty, offered the biggest smiles, and they kept saying, "Thank you Ma'am" and "Yes, Ma'am" to me. In the South, they are deliberate about teaching etiquette.

On our day off, we visited a large water park, and after a couple of hours there, a storm took us by surprise; sheets of rain blasted us, accompanied by lightning and thunder which sounded like large trees falling. Parts of the water park started flooding, before they closed the facility due to the storm. Our bus driver told me it was one of the worst storms since Hurricane Katrina.

But at night during the evening program, when students shared what the week in Mississippi meant to them so far, they did not complain about having to leave the water park.

Instead I heard: "Thank you God for that amazing storm which allowed us to get a small glimpse of what these people here have lived through, and a glimpse of Your power."

Pastor Jerry from New Covenant Community Ministries shared, that out of the Hurricane Katrina devastation, a miracle of partnership sprouted between our church and their church. He called it the Mississippi Miracle.

It's Not Random

On a Monday at about 3:30 in the afternoon, my friend Bea calls me to ask how I am doing. I say the usual "okay," and she follows it up with a "What is going on right now in your life." I tell her the obligatory things – school for the kids, sports for the kids, church for the kids, Boy Scouts for the boys, piano lessons, a recent writers conference where I was a volunteer, the house is a mess, oh, and dealing with the conflicting feeling of having two kids away at college.

Then she asks me if I had started dinner yet. That is the nagging question on every mom's mind about that time of day: What to make for dinner. I tell my friend that I have the chicken defrosting in the sink and that I am looking for my sister's recipe to make homemade enchilada sauce. I had wanted to make tortellini soup. Then she said, "Well, how about if I bring you dinner tonight?"

For me? I thought? For a family of five (well, seven, but five right now). Bringing a meal is something you do when someone is sick or has a baby or when a family member dies. But my friend insisted, "Well, God laid it on my heart to call you just now, and to offer to bring you a meal. I had made an extra white sauce lasagna casserole and I thought I would like to give it to you."

"I had a sense from the Holy Spirit that you needed to be encouraged, that perhaps you were down for some reason, and you do so much for others to make them feel special, and I just wanted to do this for you, to make you feel that you are important to so many people, especially to me."

Okay, so now I have tears welling in my eyes. Someone remembered me. And pointed out nice things about me, and wanted to do something for me, on an ordinary day.

She knew I had been having a hard time a year before when my daughter had left for Germany. An empty nest feeling, though I will have kids at home for a long while. But, things are changing with two in college and my youngest in school full time.

To have my friend think of me, to want to bring a meal to my large family, was a huge deal. And that she said God's Spirit had nudged her to do this act of kindness was especially significant to me. And even more so, that she acted on it.

How many times do we get ideas to call someone, to write a friend a note, to stop by to see a neighbor, to help a couple on the side of the road. But, we quickly talk ourselves out of it. "Oh, I'm sure they're fine." "Oh, I don't want to bother them." "They're probably busy." "I haven't talked to them in so long, it will be awkward." "I am sure they have plenty of help." "I will do it tomorrow."

I thought about the bumper sticker "Practice Random Acts of Kindness" but this kind act from my friend got me thinking about how misleading that statement actually is.

Yes, it is true that what my friend did was an act of kindness. But, it was not random.

Kindness is a fruit of the Spirit that Christians exhibit when they follow Christ and live by His Spirit.

"But the fruit of the Spirit is love, joy, peace, patience, kindness, goodness, faithfulness, gentleness and self-control. Against such things there is no law." (Galatians 5:22-23).

There was absolutely nothing random about my friend's act of kindness towards me, but instead it was an inspiration from the Spirit of God. And she listened.

I think of my friend Jeanie who began taking my kids individually during the day once a week on outings. Just because. God had laid this idea on her heart to reach out to me when I had twin babies and two others at home. There was no fanfare over what my friend was doing. It was not an "official" ministry of the church, but just something she did on her own. It was an act of kindness, an act of serving, an act of helping. And it was not random.

Like our lives should be.

THE EXTRAORDINARY ORDINARY

I wish I could leave you certain of the images in my mind, because they are so beautiful that I hate to think they will be extinguished when I am.

- Marilynne Robinson (Gilead)

Cherish the Treasures along the
Road of Life – (or, God Smiles)

It had been a year since the school shooting at Columbine High School near Littleton, Colorado. I was driving down an old tree-lined road on my way to my in-laws' home. I was in a bit of a hurry, which is not so unusual. I'm a busy mother of four children.

And there crossing the street, waddling with eight little ones behind her, was another Mama.

She, too, was in a hurry, for a different reason.

She was trying to dodge speeding cars.

I checked my rear view mirror – no one was behind me. I slowed down to a crawl, and stopped to watch this little smile from heaven.

My twin boys, who were one–and–a–half years old at the time, were unfortunately asleep in their car seats, and my school age children were at their grandparents' house where we were headed. So I had to enjoy this moment alone.

A car pulled up behind me. At first I thought the driver behind me would honk me forward, but she didn't. Instead, I saw her pointing the ducks out to her children. She was a mother enjoying a special moment with her children.

I thought about the mothers who lost children in the Colorado school shooting. They won't be able to enjoy little moments with their children any more. I felt so sad for them.

I also pondered the creek running through our backyard, where ducks come yearly to visit. Often after my daughter Rachel and oldest son Ryan get on the school bus, I tell my twin toddlers that we need to get our boots on to go feed the ducks. They get so excited. They know exactly where to go for their boots and duck food in the garage. We grab a cup full of cracked corn and meander into our backyard for a little adventure.

The stone stairs that my husband built are kid-size and lead to a little pond area in our creek where the ducks return every year. Each of my twins throws some of the corn into the water, saying "mehr" afterwards, which is German for "more."

I remember the first time wild ducks flew to our yard, when Rachel was 3-years-old and Ryan 18-months-old, and I used to walk into the backyard with them as well. They, too, enjoyed feeding our wild ducks.

We asked Rachel and Ryan back then what name we should christen our ducks, and out of the blue they came up with the names Cora and Chester. Chester happened to be a

90-year-old gentleman we used to visit and sometimes assist; he lived on Midhill Circle, which was one street over.

Every year when spring arrives, Rachel, now 9-years-old, and Ryan, 7-years-old, still get excited when Cora and Chester the ducks arrive. We are of course not sure if these are the same ducks from six years ago when ducks first arrived in our yard, but to us, they are still Cora and Chester.

Over the years, we hoped Cora and Chester would make a nest and lay eggs, and then sure enough, we found a nest in the brush and ivy vines with eight eggs in it. We were all so excited, although we never did see the ducklings. We're not sure what happened to them.

But the memories that our children are making, by experiencing simple moments of wonder with us, help give them a feeling of connectedness, of belonging, of family story.

When I was in both second and fifth grades, my family took spring trips to Austria and Germany, where my relatives live. We stayed part of the time at an old farm in Karnten, Austria with the Kanz family. Simple antiques filled the home and flowers decorated the yard while an old barn graced the property.

On one of our hikes in the Austrian woods, when I was in the fifth grade, we came upon a nest with a fawn in it; it was one of those moments you never forget. There's something beautiful about appreciating the outdoors together – whether it is baby ducks or deer. It is sometimes only a fleeting moment. Ducks fly away and baby deer grow up, as do our children. I am reminded often to take unrushed moments to appreciate the smiles from God that come our way.

May we always cherish every treasure along the way of this gift called life.

One-Year-Olds and Construction Workers

It is 85 degrees outside and we are on our way to our dentist in Gladstone. It is only a 10 minute drive, and I leave exactly 10 minutes before the 2 p.m. scheduled appointment. Plenty of time to get there with my four children, I assure myself.

But as I'm driving down Highway 43 and get near the A-Street intersection, I see traffic backed up, and I look up to see the sign, "Expect Delays."

My stress level goes up, but I smile politely at the flagger who stops the flow of cars right before I reach the one-lane traffic ahead. She returns my greeting. But inwardly, thoughts race through my mind.

"Doesn't she know that we have dentist appointments? Doesn't she know that I am a Mom of twin one-year-olds and two school age children? Couldn't she have stopped traffic at the car behind me?"

It seems like everywhere you drive there are the signs. "Detour ahead." "Slow." "Construction workers." "Merge to one lane." "Expect Delays."

I am a Mom and I don't have time for delays.

But then my thoughts are interrupted by a symphony of excited, sweet little voices that fills my van. My little one-year-old twin boys notice the back hoes, front loaders and excavators on the roadway that are the reason for my delay; and, in chorus, the twins erupt with cries of "Bagger" "Bagger" "Bagger," which is German for backhoe.

Their eyes are lit up and their arms and legs move wildly up and down as they repeat the word "Bagger" over and over and over again. They can hardly contain themselves.

The dentist would just have to wait.

This is the stuff of childhood, the mortar with which it is built. Simple joy and excitement over ordinary everyday life. To me the construction is nothing but a hassle, yet to my little boys it is an opportunity to celebrate, in this case, large work equipment.

I recently heard of an accident at a construction site where a worker was hit by a car. I do not know the details or circumstances regarding that situation, but it did make me evaluate my own driving patterns, especially when I'm running late.

Isn't it funny how when we're in a hurry, everything seems to take twice as long?

The light changes to red right when we get to the intersection. The person ahead of us is on a Sunday drive and going, well, the speed limit. The pedestrian crossing the street is walking extra slowly. The flagger stops the flow of cars right when we get to the one-lane highway.

I've been on both ends of the spectrum. Sometimes I'm the one in a hurry, and other times I'm the one who's slowing down the rest of the world.

We like to walk places in our neighborhood when we get the chance. It's fun getting out my navy blue buggy stroller and walking with the kids to rent a movie and purchase a pizza on a Friday evening. Or make our way by foot to the grocery store for a gallon of milk, and stop by to get a mocha on the way. Not worried about time.

And you can't be in a hurry.

Maybe that's why the excited sound of my children at the construction site was so refreshing. They haven't been marred by the curse of time schedules. They have all the time in the world to watch backhoes and cranes and dump trucks and front loaders and excavators.

Maybe we can learn something from them. And leave more time to get to appointments.

Thursdays with Theodore

This morning, I did not have enough eggs to make pumpkin bars, so I called my neighbor, retired Bill the fisherman, known as Grandpa Bill, asking him if he could spare some eggs. He could.

After meeting me with half a dozen eggs at the hedge which separates our homes, he says, "I'm making a fresh pot of water for tea – do you have time for a cup?"

All these thoughts ran through my head – I was making pumpkin bars for a mom who just had a baby; I had three articles I was either writing or editing; last night's dishes were still stacked in the sink; the washing machine was churning and the dryer was rumbling – Time for tea? I hesitated.

Then, Fisherman Bill said, "You're always so busy. Don't worry about it, perhaps another time."

Yes, I do feel so busy, like any mom, and I wish I had three more hours a day. But I did not want Bill the fisherman to think I had no time for him, and I realized at that moment that we have to make deliberate times for tea with the neighbors.

So I told Grandpa Bill that I was not too busy, but that I needed to get a few things done first and then I would come over. And Thursdays, it was a tradition to have fish sandwiches for lunch at Bill's, where he tells me stories of fishing and being a truck driver and his German friends in Canada who fish with him.

We should always have time for tea – and lunch – with our neighbors. While they are still around. Bill has since passed away.

Roberta, our elderly neighbor on the other side of us, is not around anymore either. When we moved into our home on View Drive in 1989, I was pregnant with our first child, Rachel; and Roberta was out walking up the gravel driveway in her robe to get the morning newspaper. She was the first neighbor we met on View Drive.

Time stood still when you visited Roberta. I'd meander down her path, our two young children in tow, to see her or to return her dog that used to wander the streets. She told tales of adding on to her home and how hers was the only house on the block for years. Sometimes she would say, "You don't visit me very often" and I felt guilty when she would say that to me.

One day Roberta got sick and moved to a retirement home; and now she's gone.

I think to myself, if we don't have time to visit our neighbors then we are surely missing something of value in life.

I remember being in Germany with my grandma Omi in Bad Homburg, and we'd take the bus to the woods every day to hike; during our walk, we'd stop at cafes that were located in the middle of the woods to sip coffee and eat Torte.

When our family lived in Corvallis, Oregon during my early grade school days, my brother and sister and I as well as my friend Jeanie visited two different ladies that we called the Neighbor Ladies. We'd stop by unannounced and they'd give us cookies. And, I enjoy returning to Jeanie's parents' house in the country every year with my children. They somehow represent a simpler way of life.

I love taking the time to go to my sister's house in the summer; we sip ice tea on her deck while our kids play in the yard, or we'll go on hikes in the woods and let the kids run. And I enjoy walks with my parents. In the past I used to go on bicycle rides with my father. Due to health issues now, he is not able to ride his bike anymore.

This past summer while driving the kids to catch the bus for Tilikum church camp, we saw this older gentleman wearing a red hat sitting in his lawn chair near the road in front of his home, waving, and I'd purposely slow down and wave back. And we saw him the next day, both before and after camp, smiling and waving. And I'd ponder if he looked at me as a speeding mom rushing through life. And I'd wonder about this man's story.

One day, we were once again driving past the same older gentleman wearing his red hat while he waved at passersby, and I told my children that we should stop to say hello sometime. But we had dinner to make and places to go and things to do and life to live. But the thought did not go away. Is that from God? Dinner could wait.

I got my children out of the car and we went to introduce ourselves to this gentleman who waved daily to passersby. His name is Theodore. He is in his late 80's, a former music teacher. And he said he decided to sit in the mornings and the evenings near the road on the sidewalk to greet people as they traveled to and from work. No, he was not trying to slow folks down as I had first thought. No, he was not judging moms for being in a hurry. He was just being a friendly smiling face.

He shared the story of one day holding a sign announcing his birthday. Within the next 24 hours, he received over 30 cards from people. And even a bottle of wine, but he doesn't drink so he gave that back. He takes the time to make people happy. I decided that summer to try to visit him once a week on Thursdays.

I called it Thursdays with Theodore.

The Extraordinary Ordinary

I am so loving having my 19-year-old daughter Rachel home for the summer after she was in Europe at Bible school for nine months. I rise several days a week at the crack of dawn to ride my bicycle with her to her job six miles away, where she works for Clackamas County.

I cherish our morning bicycle rides. The sunrise is splendid. The fresh air, the conversation, the everyday feel of life, the moment, the wonder, the sweetness of having this time with my daughter. I thank God for what some view as ordinary, but to me it's extraordinary.

Several of the days that we ride together, I take her out for mochas at an independent coffee shop near her work in Oregon City. I plan it. I call it our morning summer tradition.

I want her to remember this time. At the coffee shop, we find comfortable chairs to sit in and we talk about life. Family and church and faith and school and frustrations and the future and careers and passions and callings and health and relationships and American culture compared with German culture and community.

Daily conversations, moments with people, with family, with friends. You have to be there for them. To be available. Forget just quality time. We need time. There is no substitute. And time is what I love having for my family. Taking the time. To sit after dinner to talk instead of rushing off to do work. To make tea in the evenings, then sit on the deck or the couch to sip and see who will join you. To enjoy the extraordinary ordinary.

On a particular evening where I had a commitment to go to a writers meeting I lead at church, I realized that I did not want to miss out on what was happening at home. Rachel's friend had come over, and I had initially thought they were going to go out.

But when they sat at the island in our kitchen and I offered them ice tea and then dinner, to my surprise they said they'd like to stay for a meal. I had not even made dinner, but I quickly scrambled and figured something out. I wanted it to be nice for my daughter and her friend. I wanted to give them a reason to stay for the evening, though I would not be there for part of it.

I began looking for what to make for dinner. We had plenty of vegetables, perfect basics to add to pasta. As I began to place zucchini, tomatoes, onions, garlic, mushrooms, and spinach on the island, Rachel joined me in chopping up summer's bounty. I love cooking with her. I enjoy cooking with all of my children. And, now Rachel enjoys making meals and desserts for others.

After making dinner and setting the table, I hurried off to my meeting, but returned in a timely manner. I did not want to be gone for the ordinary every day moment of being together that evening.

It is important to be deliberate about creating a welcoming home. A place that is not rushed, a place where our children can talk about life and God and faith and worries and questions and dreams and friendships and everyday life. A place where our children can laugh and be silly and be themselves.

I remember walking one morning to the local Sourdough Willy's bakery to purchase sticky buns and apricot and cream cheese danishes with my oldest son, Ryan, who was 17 at the time, and my youngest son Augustin, who was 6-years-old. Ryan was chasing his baby brother Augustin down the street, and Augustin was running away and laughing and giggling. And when Ryan caught his brother, he scooped him up and hugged him and said "I caught you, I'm faster than you are," and Augustin bounced right back and said, "No you are not," and he somehow wriggled his way down and began running away from his big brother again. And the entire walk with my two deep-dark-brown-eyed boys was pure beauty.

Seeing our children absorbed in one another and in family life; like Rachel planting an herb garden with her baby brother in the summer. Like her taking each of her four brothers out on special one on one dates when she is home: on bicycle rides to Moon Struck Chocolate for mocha milkshakes and on long walks to Coffee Nook for espresso mocha smoothies. Like Ryan wrestling with his twin brothers in the living room.

The loveliness of everyday life surrounds me. Like the conversations during family road trips and at campground campfires. Like hikes in the woods with our children dashing after anything that moves. Like all seven of us sitting in the sanctuary at church together. Like gathering around the dinner table. I offer thanks to God for these moments in our family's life; moments that are prayers and poetry and grace and hope. And extraordinary.

About The Author

Cornelia Becker Seigneur was born in Germany, and raised in the States by her professor father and her school teacher/stockbroker/stay-at-home mother, both German immigrants. Cornelia graduated from Cleveland High School in Portland, Oregon and attended Reed College for a year. She earned her Bachelor of Arts in English degree from the University of Portland, where she met her future husband Chris while they were both student leaders with Campus Crusade for Christ. They now live in West Linn, Oregon and have five children, ages 7 to 20, including a set of identical twin boys. They are active in community outreach and at Rolling Hills Community Church while also enjoying Imago Dei Community. Cornelia's Master of Arts in German degree is from Portland State University.

Cornelia is an adjunct instructor at Multnomah University in Portland, Oregon, and she has also taught at George Fox University, among other higher education settings. She has been a freelance journalist for The Oregonian newspaper since 1996, specializing in faith, family, and community features. She penned the Real-Life Mom column there for three years. Her writing has been featured on CNN and Fox News, among other outlets and publications. Besides WriterMom Tales, Cornelia is the author of *Images of America: WEST LINN*. She's also been a school teacher, editor, and church youth director.

Cornelia has continued in youth ministry at church over the years, leading Bible studies, serving as a camp counselor, and assisting with youth mission trips. She has a heart for missions and Sudan refugees in the Portland area. Cornelia has completed six marathons, the most recent one the 2009 Portland Marathon. She also likes hiking, camping, bicycle riding, reading, and going on adventures with her family.

Cornelia enjoys speaking to church groups, at writing conferences, in schools, and to community service organizations. Her website and blog are www.corneliaseigneur.com

The author and her family on a summer 2009 camping road trip vacation to Yellowstone National Park.

LaVergne, TN USA
01 October 2010
199290LV00001B/20/P